Study of Adverbs, Prepositions, Conjunctions & Interjections

Classifications, Forms & Formation, Adverbial Function of Prepositions, Role of Conjunctions to form Sentences & different Interjections.

Mr. Peter

DEDICATION

Dedicated to my children, Nicky & Om

Writer's Academic works:

1. Study of Nouns, Pronouns, Adjectives & Articles (detail study) ISBN: 979-842-211-856-4 / 979-888-704-109-4
2. All about Verbs (Forms, Functions, Conjugation, Tense, Voice Change, Forming Questions & Negation) ISBN: 979-840-441-149-2 / 979-888-704-411-8
3. Study of Adverbs, Prepositions, Conjunctions & Interjections ISBN: 979-840-785-010-6 / 979-888-704-532-0
4. Detail Study of Phrases, Clauses & Sentences, including Idioms & Phrasal Verbs ISBN: 979-840-881-405-3 / 979-888-704-582-5
5. Study of Subject-Verb Agreement, Narration Change, Use of Punctuation; including Analysis, Synthesis & Split-up (Study through charts, division, explanation and examples) ISBN: 979-880-723-013-3 / 979-888-704-674-7
6. **Peter's 'English Grammar, A Complete Version of English Grammar,** (detail study, explanation & examples) ISBN: 979-879-725-020-3 / 979-888-704-463-7
7. **Question Bank of English Grammar & Composition (Learn through Exercises)** ISBN: 979-883-531-890-2 / 979-888-733-132-4
8. **Rhetoric & Prosody** (A handbook of Figures of Speech, rhymes, feet of poetic lines for High School Students) ISBN: 979-840-526-645-9 / 979-888-684-952-3
9. Picture Composition; For Primary Level, Std-I to V (Development of Writing Skill from Single Sentence Formation to Paragraph Writing, incl. question patterns and answer guide) ISBN: 979-888-805-249-5 (B&W) / 979-888-783-066-7 (color print)
10. Steps to Composition (Development of Writing Skill, Part-1), includes Picture Composition, Essay & Story Writing ISBN: 979-884-408-069-2 / 979-888-805-001-9
11. Development of Writing Skill, Part-2 (includes Letter Writing- Business Letters, Application for Jobs, Letters to Editor, bank authorities, Institutional Heads & others) ISBN: 979-835-689-886-0 / 979-888-833-455-3
12. Development of Writing Skill, Part-3 (includes- E-mails, Poster Making, Notices, Processing, Dialogue, Article, Speech & Debate Writing as well as Diary entry, Summary and Reporting) ISBN: 979-836-392-249-7 / 979-888-869-544-9
13. **A Book of Advanced Writing Skill, the Complete Version** (incl Part-1, 2 & 3) ISBN: 979-836-472-826-5 / 979-888-869-835-8

Author page URL's:

https://www.amazon.com/author/mr.peter

https://www.amazon.in/~/e/B09QW2P4TY *(For Indians, this and next)*

https://notionpress.com/store/s?NP_Books%5Bquery%5D=Mr.+Peter

https://www.amazon.co.uk/~/e/B09QW2P4TY

https://www.amazon.de/~/e/B09QW2P4TY

https://www.amazon.fr/~/e/B09QW2P4TY

https://www.amazon.co.jp/~/e/B09QW2P4TY

https://www.amazon.es/~/e/B09QW2P4TY

https://www.amazon.it/~/e/B09QW2P4TY

https://www.amazon.com.br/kindle-dbs/entity/author?asin=B09QW2P4TY

For Readers from India and nearby, you may place order with notionpress.com

Visit notionpress.com and type 'Mr. Peter' in the search box; give order of books to **avail elegant discounts** *using the following* **Coupon Codes;** as, unique00, bulk00, Deal1 and so on against the books: (if not work, contact to https://www.facebook.com/profile.php?id=100081822070172 or (5) Books Campaigns, Free Coupons, Learning English Grammar & Composition | Facebook

Coupon Codes	Book Name	Buy for	Discount %	Rebate Prices
unique00	**Advanced Writing Skill, the Complete Version** (incl. Part-1, 2 & 3)	1 copy	15	~~780~~ 663
PujaDeal10	Development of Writing Skill, Part-3	1 copy	18	~~365~~ 300
PujaDeal9	Development of Writing Skill, Part-2	1 copy	18	~~365~~ 300
PujaDeal8	Steps to Composition (Development	1 copy	20	~~300~~ 240

Study of Adverbs, Prepositions, Conjunctions & Interjections

	of Writing Skill, Part-1)			
PujaDeal7	**Rhetoric & Prosody**	1 copy	20	~~240~~ 192
PujaDeal6	**Question Bank of English Grammar & Composition**	1 copy	20	~~559~~ 448
PujaDeal5	Study of Subject-Verb Agreement, Narration Change, Use of Punctuation; including Analysis, Synthesis & Split-up	1 copy	20	~~301~~ 241
PujaDeal4	Detail Study of Phrases, Clauses & Sentences, including Idioms & Phrasal Verbs	1 copy	20	~~290~~ 232
PujaDeal3	Study of Adverbs, Prepositions, Conjunctions & Interjections	1 copy	20	~~260~~ 208
PujaDeal2	All about Verbs (Forms, Functions, Conjugation, Tense, Voice Change, Forming Questions & Negation)	1 copy	18	~~420~~ 345
PujaDeal1	Study of Nouns, Pronouns, Adjectives & Articles (detail study)	1 copy	20	~~280~~ 224
unique01	**Peter's 'English Grammar'** (Complete Version of English Grammar)	1 copy	23	~~1201~~ 925
	FOR COPIES MORE THAN ONE			
bulk00	**Advanced Writing Skill, the Complete Version** (incl. Part-1, 2 & 3)	2 to 5000 copies	23	~~780~~ 601
Deal11	Development of Writing Skill, Part-3	2 to 5000 copies	24	~~365~~ 278
Deal10	Development of Writing Skill, Part-2	2 to 5000 copies	24	~~365~~ 278
Deal9	Steps to Composition (Development of Writing Skill, from Primary to Secondary Level)	2 to 5000 copies	26	~~300~~ 222
Deal8	**Rhetoric & Prosody**	2 to 5000 copies	26	~~240~~ 178
Deal7	**Question Bank of English Grammar & Composition**	2 to 5000 copies	28	~~559~~ 403
bulk01	**Peter's 'English Grammar'** (Complete Version of English Grammar)	2 to 5000 copies	30	~~1201~~ 841
Deal5	Study of Subject-Verb Agreement, Narration Change, Use of Punctuation; including Analysis, Synthesis & Split-up	2 to 5000 copies	26	~~301~~ 223
Deal4	Detail Study of Phrases, Clauses & Sentences, including Idioms & Phrasal Verbs	2 to 5000 copies	26	~~290~~ 215
Deal3	Study of Adverbs, Prepositions, Conjunctions & Interjections	2 to 5000 copies	26	~~260~~ 193
Deal2	All about Verbs (Forms, Functions, Conjugation, Tense, Voice Change, Forming Questions & Negation)	2 to 5000 copies	26	~~420~~ 311
Deal1	Study of Nouns, Pronouns, Adjectives & Articles (detail study)	2 to 5000 copies	26	~~280~~ 208

CONTENTS

Preface

The book in its little span of space, covers detail study of four pillars of the parts of speech, i.e., **Adverbs, Prepositions, Conjunctions & Interjections**; when other four have already taken their place in two separate books and all together share their place in the complete version of English Grammar by Mr. Peter.

However, the present book deals of definition, classification, forms and formation in details of the four., including ample examples for each section, suitable for high school students to comprehend. The book **'Study of Adverbs, Prepositions, Conjunctions & Interjections',** besides dealing in details of Adverbs, also includes account of Degrees, Forms & Formation, Position of Adverbs in sentences; it provides space for discussion of Adverbial Function of Prepositions, shows us the Role of Conjunctions and gives us abundant examples how different Interjections express diverse emotions and the feelings of a speaker.

1. Adverbs, Kinds (16) & Their Uses

○ There are more than **'16' kinds of adverbs** present in English grammar which are <u>grouped in '3' main classes</u>. **However**, we will discuss this chapter under the following heads:

    A.   Definition & Classification,
    B.   Illustration of Simple Adverbs (14 in numbers),
    C.   Relative Adverbs &
    D.   Interrogative Adverbs;
    E.   Degree & Comparison,
    F.   Forms & Formation of Adverbs &
    G.   The Position of Adverbs in the sentence.

Definition & Classification of Adverb

○ <u>Study the following sentences.</u>

    1) Peter **runs**.
    2) He runs *fast*.
    3) He runs *very* fast.
    4) It is a **mango**.
    5) It is a **sweet** mango.
    6) The mango is *very* sweet.
    7) I have read *all* <u>through this book</u>.
    8) *Unfortunately,* <u>no one was present there</u>.
    9) This is the reason *why* I left her.
    10) *When* did he come?

Explanation

1) <u>In sentence-1,</u> '**runs**' is a verb which shows an activity of Peter. It tells us, what Peter does.

2) <u>In sentence-2,</u> '*fast*' adds meaning to the verb 'runs. How does he run? = *fast*.

3) <u>In sentence-3,</u> the word '*very*' adds meaning to the word 'fast'. How fast does he run? = *very* fast.

4) <u>The sentence-4</u> is a statement which tells us a name of a fruit, = <u>a</u> <u>mango.</u> The 'mango' is a noun. (However, here the word 'mango' <u>is a complement to the verb 'is'</u>).

5) <u>In sentence-5,</u> the word '**sweet**' describes the noun, so it is an Adjective, but

6) In sentence-6, the word '***very***' adds meaning to the adjective 'sweet'. How sweet is the mango? = *very*.

7) In sentence-7, the word '***all***' adds meaning to the phrase 'through this book'. How much have you read? = **all** through this book, refers 'degree of quantity'.

8) In sentence-8, the word '***unfortunately***' adds meaning to whole sentence following it 'no one was present there'. 'Unfortunately,' is an adverb, modifying the verb 'being present'.

9) In sentence-9, the word '***why***' joins the two clauses, besides, modifying the clause, 'I left her' or to the verb sense 'leaving her'. 'Why' is a relative adverb.

10) In sentence-10, the word '***when***' is used to ask question, and its answers are always simple adverbs. Here: 'when did he come?' = *yesterday at 9 p.m./in the morning/ in the evening/ at night*, etc. are the examples of adverbial phrases, denoting 'time' & '**when**' is an Interrogative Adverb. **All the italic & bold** words are the examples of adverbs in the sentences.

The Definition: An adverb is a word that generally modifies or adds meaning to a ***verb***, or an ***adjective***, or an ***adverb***, *and often **a phrase** or **a sentence** using at the beginning of them (clause or sentence).* Besides, an adverb is also used to ***join clauses*** & to ***ask questions*** like in the above sentences.

✱ **Note**: The above definition itself reflects different roles of an adverb in the sentence. It has mainly four parts—

(1) modifying a verb, an adjective or an adverb (which are single words;

(2) it may modify also a phrase or a sentence too;

(3) Besides modifying words, phrase or sentence, it also joins clauses (the function of Relative Adverbs like a Relative Pronoun), and

(4) To ask questions (the function of Interrogative Adverb); thereby we may find out simple adverbs from the sentence.

A **Relative adverb** joins two clauses, refers **place, reason, time**, etc, doing the function of an adverb, *but introduce always a relative or adjective clause in the sentence*. Study examples.
Answers to Interrogative adverb are always the simple adverbs.
The answers may be an **adverb of time, place, reason, cause, purpose** or any other.

Study the examples:
1) The engineer worked **carefully** on the engine.

* How did he work? =carefully, refers 'manner'.

2) Ruby is a **very** <u>good</u> student.
   * How good? =very good, refers the degree.

3) He left the place **quite** <u>suddenly</u>.
   * How did he leave the place? = suddenly, refers the 'degree' of manner)

   * <u>Read also others:</u>

4) She was sitting ***close*** <u>beside him</u>. (Where, refers place)

5) She lives ***far*** <u>of us</u>. (Where, refers distance of place)

6) At what hours is the sun ***right*** <u>above us</u>? (Where, refers the point of position; 'at what hours?'--the answer of the question will be the adverb of time; as, = at 12 pm.)

7) The tiger was ***just*** <u>behind us</u> howling. (Where, refers the point of position.)

8) The building was ***in the right*** <u>of the Post Office</u>. (Where, in which side, refers the direction.)

9) Have you read ***all*** <u>through this book</u>? (How much have you read this book? = all through this book, refers degree of quantity.)

10) She was dressed ***all*** <u>in pink</u>. ('in pink' itself is the phrase of adjective refers the color, and the phrase is modified by the adverb 'all'. How much pink? = all, refers the degree of color.)

11) He paid his debts ***down*** <u>to the last penny</u>. (The bold word refers manner, while the phrase, 'to the last penny' refers the degree.)

12) He *slowly* sipped his wine ***all*** <u>to the bottom</u>. (The phrase, 'to the bottom' refers quantity, while the bold word 'all' refers the degree of that quantity, and slowly refers the manner of sipping' his wine in the sentence.)

All the above underlined are the examples of phrases, modified by the adverbs, preceding them & written in bold, in the sentences.

Adverbs also modify a Sentence or **a Clause** using before them; as in the above by **'all'**, **'down'**, etc.

<u>Adverbs standing at the beginning of sentences sometimes modify the whole sentences</u>, rather than any particular word; as,

13) **Probably** <u>he is mistaken</u>. (The state or the condition is 'he is mistaken', and by the word 'probably' the condition is modified, which is a sentence. Thus, the sense is 'It is that he is mistaken to be a doctor., when he may not be so.)

14) **Possible** it is as you said. (It is possible what you said to be true or not be true.)
15) **Certainly,** you are wrong. (It is certain that you are wrong.)
16) **Evidently** the figures are incorrect. (It is evident that the figures are incorrect.)
17) **Unfortunately,** no one was present there. (No one was present there & it was unfortunate.)
18) **Luckily,** he escaped unhurt. (He was lucky that he escaped unhurt.)

- All the above underlined are the examples of clauses or sentence, modified by the adverbs in bold, used in the beginning of the sentences, being themselves parts of the sentences or clauses.

Classification of Adverbs

The following is the chart of the division of adverbs, which are put into three main classes. Together they are sixteen in number.

Study the chart carefully:

Kinds of Adverbs		
Simple adverbs	**Relative** or Wh-Adjunctive **Adverbs**	**Interrogative adverbs**
The simple adverbs are used to modify meanings of a verb, or an adjective, or an adverb, or a phrase, clause or sentence. **They are fourteen in number.**	Where adverbs besides modifying, relate or refer back to their antecedents & thereby do join clauses. These are also some 'wh' words; as, why, when, where, how, in what manner, how long, how much, how often, etc. **Read the examples:**	Where adverbs are used to ask questions with 'wh' words- why, when, where, how, in what manner, how long, how much, how often, etc., and their answers are mostly simple adverbs (denoting **time. place, reason, result**, or other); as,
1) Time, 2) Frequency, 3) Place, 4) Movement or direction, 5) Manner, 6) Affirmation, 7) Negation,	1) Tell them the reason *why* I came. 2) I know the street *where* the bank is. 3) This was the reason *why* I left her.	1) Where is your Ram? 2) Why are you late? 3) How did you do it? 4) How much work can you do in a day? 5) How high is the

8) Reason or Cause, 9) Purpose & Result, 10) Conditions, 11) Concession or Compromise 12) Certainty, 13) Focusing, 14) Degree or Quantity;	4) I remember the house *where* I was born. 5) Tell us the time *when* you will come. 6) Tell her *how much* you love her. If can't, just shut-up before us.	Kutub Minar? 6) When will he arrive tomorrow? 7) How often did she come? 8) How much she loved you. 9) In what manner you did it.

Note: The relative adverbs & the interrogative adverbs are mostly same in form. They are both are the 'wh' words. The difference lies in their uses only. The relative adverbs are used to join clauses, and they, like relative adjectives or pronouns, relate or refer back to their antecedents to show 'relation' and introduce always 'Relative Clauses'. Whereas, the interrogative adverbs are used to ask questions to find Simple Adverbs.

Simple Adverbs (14 in numbers)

In use, adverbs may group into 3 major classes; however, in meaning, they are '16' or more in number (kinds). Study them now one by one.

(1) **Adverb of Time**

Adverbs of Time: the adverbs or adverb phrases which show 'when'; when an action is being done/takes place/happens.
1) We have seen the film **before**.
2) I have heard this **before**.
3) We shall **now** begin to work.
4) I had a letter from him **lately**.
5) I have spoken to him **already**.
6) Mr. Gupta **formerly** lived here.
7) That day he arrived **late**.
8) The end came **soon**.
9) A year ***hence*** (after a length of time in the future), it will be forgotten by everybody here present.
10) Wasted time **never** returns.
11) The train has **already** left the station.
12) We moved into our new house **last week**.
13) Our favorite T.V. program starts **at 6'o clock**.

14) I'm going to join my new school **tomorrow**.
15) He once met me in Cairo; I have not seen him **since**.
16) He went away two hours ***ago***.
17) I will do it ***soon***.
18) The boy arrived ***late*** in class.
19) He has ***already*** arrived.

✖ Adverb of Time answer the questions, 'when'/at what time?

(2) **Adverb of Frequency**

Adverb of Frequency: The adverb or adverb phrases which answer to the questions, 'how often' or 'how many times' an action is done:

1) I have told you ***twice***.
2) I have not seen him ***once*** since then.
3) He ***often*** makes mistakes.
4) He ***seldom*** comes here.
5) The postman called ***again***.
6) He ***always*** tries to do his best.
7) He ***frequently*** comes unprepared.
8) Our children ***always*** go to school on the bus.
9) I'll ***never*** make that mistake ***again***.
10) I clean my bedroom ***every day***.
11) Dad polishes his shoes ***twice a week***.
12) He ***often*** makes mistakes.
13) I used to watch movies ***twice*** a week.
14) She ***seldom*** writes me.
15) I ***always*** wake up early in the morning.
16) ***Firstly***, mangoes are bought from market.
17) ***Sometimes*** an ignorant also works excellent.
18) He comes here ***daily***.
19) He ***occasionally*** visits the place.
20) She began to call ***daily***.

✖ Adverb of Frequency answers to the question, 'how often'/how many times?

(3) **Adverb of Place or Position**

Adverb of Place: the adverb or adverb phrases that show 'where'/ 'at what place' an action happens or takes place.

1) The boys are playing ***upstairs***.
2) The dog is ***<u>in the garden</u>***.
3) We're going ***to New York City*** on our school trip.
4) It's very sunny but cold ***outside***.
5) Stand ***here***. Go ***there***. Walk ***backward***.
6) The little lamb follows Mary ***everywhere***.
7) He looked ***up***. My brother is ***out***.
8) Is Mr. Das is ***within***? Come ***in***.
9) The horse galloped ***away***.
10) Stop **here**. Go **there**. Come **in**.
11) The teacher is **out**. The doctor is **in.**
12) He fell **down**. The rust is **everywhere**.
13) Go **inside**. Get **out**. The bird flies **upward**.
14) He gets **<u>into the train</u>**. He works **<u>at an office</u>**, etc.

- Adverb of Place answer the questions- 'Where?'

(4) <u>Adverb of Movement or Direction</u>

- The adverbs or adverb phrases that show 'direction'/ 'movement of an action' are called the **adverb of Movement** or **Direction**. *The Adverb of Movement or Direction may be included in the class of Adverb of Place, for they also denote location.*
  - It answers to the questions '<u>where to</u>', '<u>what along</u>', *<u>to which direction or place</u>*' or '*<u>from where</u>*'; as

1) They are running ***towards the city***. (Where are they running to?)
2) They are walking along ***the road/along the sea beach***. (What along are they walking?)
3) We moved ***forward.*** They moved ***northward.*** (To which direction did they move?)
4) These were falling ***from the top.*** (From where were these falling?)
5) He is coming ***hither*** (to this place). (Where is he coming to?)
6) ***Hither*** he is coming, everyone be alert.
7) ***Thither*** (to/towards that place) she is going, keep watch on her. (Where to is she going?)
8) People began rushing ***hither & thither***. (Also, hither & yon) (where to did they begin to rush?)

Whither = where/ to which place; used to ask what is likely to happen to something in the future.

9) **Whither** should they go? They did not know **whither** (*what place*) to go.
10) **Whither** modern architecture will go after this decade?
11) **Whither** modern technology do, let us know in the seminar.
12) Get thee **hence** (*from here, from this place*), Satan! (Where to go for Satan?)
13) I am going **hence** (*going from here?*) to my own land.
14) They made their way from Spain to France & **thence** (*from that place*) to England. (Where to go from France?)
15) He was promoted to manager, **thence** (*from that position or situation*) to a partnership in the farm.
16) The aliens returned **whence** (*from where*) they had come. (Where did they return to?)

(5) **Adverb of Manner or Means**

Adverb of Manner/Means: It shows '*how*' or '*in what way or manner*' *something happens or is done*; as,

1) Soumya reads **clearly**.
2) The letter is **well** written.
3) This story reads **well**.
4) The plane landed **smoothly**.

5) The child slept **soundly**.
6) Slowly and **sadly,** we laid him down.
7) You should not do **so**.
8) The Sikhs fought **bravely**.
9) The boy works **hard**.
10) I was **agreeably** disappointed. Is that **so**?
11) **Thus** only, will you succeed?
12) The girls answered all the questions **correctly**.
13) He was driving **carelessly**.

14) Ramu plays guitar **skillfully**.
15) He <u>spoke</u> **confidently**.
16) Mampi <u>sits</u> **silently** besides me.
17) The bus <u>runs</u> **soundly** on the road.
18) The train <u>runs</u> **slowly**.
19) The leader said all that **wisely**.
20) Nick spoke something, I could not hear **clearly**.
21) They did the task **rapidly**.
22) He fell down **suddenly** and died **instant** giving us no time to take him to the nearby hospital **even**.
23) Thus, one's end may come **by chance**, and we *hardly* get time to think over **even** on the eternal truths of life.

However, here the mentioned adverb '**hardly**' is an **adverb of negation**' and '**by chance**' is often termed as '**time**' rather than be an adverb of manner.

(6) **Adverb of Affirmation &**
(7) **Adverb of Negation**

The adverbs that say—yes, certainly, definitely, surely, etc. which denote *affirmation or certainty of something to happen*, *refer acceptance*, etc. are called the Adverbs of Affirmation, and the adverbs that says— no, not, never, none, perhaps, probably, etc., *which denote negation or no to something to do,* or *refer denying,* etc., are called the Adverbs of Negation.

The Words that refer Negation & Affirmation
(Remember, all are not Adverbs)

Words of **Negation**	Words of **Affirmation**
No, Not, Never, No longer, No more, Nothing, Not a bit, Nobody/None/ No one,	Yes, of course, certainly, definitely, surely, only, any, all, some, ever, always,
Nowhere, Nothing but, Scarcely, Hardly, Rarely= 15	something, anything somewhere, anywhere = (15)

Ways, how Adverb of Affirmation or Negation comes out as answer to the questions with 'Verb '**To Be**', '**To Have**', '**To Do**' or by any other helping verb, like 'modals':

→ Are you a man? =**Of course**, why not?
→ Is she your girlfriend? =**No**, she is not.
→ Have you seen the film? = **Yes**, I have.
→ Have you written her? = **No**, I haven't.
→ Do you know him? = **Yes**.
→ Do you want this? = **No**, thanks.
→ Will you go there? = **Certainly**, I will.
→ Should I go? =**Definitely** not. / **Sure**.

The adverbs **which affirm** or say **'yes'** to some action; as,
1) Have you got it? = **Yes.** I have got it.
2) ***Surely*** you are mistaken.
3) He ***certainly*** went there.
4) **Yes, *of course*,** you ***must*** do it. ('must' is a modal. The modals are mostly used like an adverb, add meaning to the verb. For details, read the chapter of Modals.)
5) ***Certainly,*** they did it.
6) ***Surely*** go there & tell him to flee.
7) I drink ***all*** to the bottom.
8) He ***ever*** asks me of my name.
9) Go ***anywhere. Only*** do_n't_ ask me _again_ this matter.
10) ***Somewhere*** it was lost, and ***somewhere*** it was found.

The adverbs which say **'no'** or **'not'** to certain action; 'denies something' or introduce negation in the sense; as,

1) Have you done it? = **No.** I have **not** done it. Is he busy? = **No**, he is **not**.
2) I do **not** know him.
3) Things are **no** better at present.
4) **No longer** has he lived. **No longer** does she live.
5) **Never** come here.
6) I have **not** any car.
7) He remained of **nowhere**.
8) **Scarcely** had they liked us.
9) **Scarcely** had she love for me. (Here: had is used as main verb, and 'love' is a noun)
10) **Hardly** had we listened to her shout for help last night. **Hardly** did we hear her.
11) **Rarely** there was a sit for us. *All* were *merely* booked.

Note: _No longer_, _scarcely_, _hardly_—**generally are used in perfect tenses** and _has, have, had_ or _any other helping verb_ (if not perfect tense) follow the words as in the above sentences.

(8) Adverbs of reason or cause

The adverb which tells about a reason or cause of an action done or to happen is called the adverb of Reason or Cause. They are introduced by the following sub-ordinate conjunctions; as, – *because, as, since, hence, etc.,* and answer to the question 'why'?

1) He cannot come, **because** he is ill. (Why can't he come?)
2) **As** he is ill, he cannot come.
3) **Since** you are ill, you need not come. (Why need I not come?)
4) I am sorry **that** you said this. (Why do you feel sorry?)
5) I am going hence (from here), **because** you have insulted me. (Why are you going?)
6) **As** he did the offence, he is unable to refute the charge. (Why is he unable to refute the charge?)

(9) Adverb of Purpose & Result

Adverb of Purpose: The adverb of purpose are introduced by the following sub-ordinate conjunctions, like that of Result; as, – *that, in order that, so that, lest,* etc.

1) We read **_that_** *(for the purpose that/in the result of)* we may learn.
2) He works hard **_in order that /so that_** he may succeed.
3) Walk slowly and carefully **_lest_** *(in order somebody not) you* fall in the ditch.
4) She studied hard **_so that_** he would pass in the examination.

The relative pronouns— **_who, which_** —make relative or adjective clauses in the sentences but they may refer both cause or purpose. Read the chart.

Relative clause but refer Cause	Relative clause but referring Purpose
• My brother **_who_** *(because he) is ill* cannot come. • The picture **_which_** *(because it) was spoiled*, has been thrown away. *Note:* In the above sentences, the sub-ordinate clauses — 'who is ill' & 'which was spoilt'— both are the relative clauses; they have described their antecedent nouns— 'brother' & 'picture' respectively; but the words 'who' meaning = *because he/she* & 'which' meaning = *because it* are the adverbs, denoting cause'.	• I shall send my brother **_who_** *(that he may)* will do the work. • I have bought a dog **_which_** *(in order that it)* would guard my house at night. *Note:* In the above sentences, the sub-ordinate clauses — 'who will do the work' & 'which would guard my house at night'—both are the sub-ordinate relative clauses; they have described their antecedent nouns— 'brother' & 'dog' respectively; but the words 'who' meaning = *that he may* & 'which' meaning = *in order that it* are the adverbs, denoting 'purpose'.

Adverb of Result

The adverb of result often may be treated as differently from the adverb of purpose. In that case, one number might be added to fourteen to be fifteen Simple Adverbs. *The Adverb of Result is that*

<u>refers to result or outcome of an action</u>.

The adverbs of result are introduced by the following sub-ordinate conjunctions; as, – *that, so that, such that, therefore, hence,* etc.
1)   I am so tired ***that*** (in the result of) I can't walk.
2)   *What have I done **that** (in the result of) you desert me?*
3)   *He is <u>such</u> a fool **that** (as a result of) I can't depend on him.*
4)   He did the offence; ***hence*** (for this reason/as a result of) he is unable to refute the charge. (What is the result of his doing offence?)
5)   He was ill treated by all for his caste. He ***therefore*** left the school. (What happened that he was ill-treated in the school?)
6)   *I wanted to buy a book; **therefore**, I had gone there.* (What did you do to buy a book?)

Sometimes, '**that**' is understood (omitted); and in place of '**that**' we use **comma** (,) like in the following sentences:
7)   He is so weak, he can't walk.
8)   You were so late; I could not wait.

(10)   Adverb of Condition or Supposition

○   The <u>adverbs that refer to condition (supposition, provision or situation)</u> for an action to happen, is called the adverb of ***Condition or Supposition.***

They are introduced by the following sub-ordinate conjunctions; as, – **if, unless, in case, whether, on condition, provided (that), supposing that,** *etc.*
1)   ***If*** I succeed, I shall help you.
2)   I shall not go ***unless*** you come.
3)   I may come in; ***in case*** I have time.
4)   He will come ***provided*** he gets leave.
5)   I shall try, ***whether*** I succeed or not.
6)   ***Had I been*** (If I had been) rich, I would help you.
7)   ***Were I*** (If I were) present there, I would oppose to that proposal.

○   **Compare: Adverbs of Reason, Result & Condition**

Adv. Of Reason	Adv. Of Result	Adv. Of Condition

• **Because of** I doubtlessly believe her, I gave her the attorney power. • **Because** she played the day long, she didn't stand first in her Examination. • **As** he failed to catch the train, he was late in the meeting. • **As** I worked very hard, good was my result.	• She was always lazy; **consequently,** she didn't get any job in her life time. • She is not studying well, **so** she'll not stand 1st position in the Exam. • He failed the train, **hence/therefore** *(for the reason, as a result)* he was late. • I worked very hard, **accordingly** good was my result in all exams.	• **Even if** none loves you, you should not hate them. • **Even** I had insulted you, you offered your help. • **Unless** you start now, you will miss the train. • **If** I didn't work very hard, I missed my position at any time.

(11)   **Adverbs of Concession or Compromise**

○ **The adverbs of Condition** & the **adverbs of Concession** are honestly to say are same and not different.

The adverb that refers to <u>concession</u> or <u>compromise</u> *which often refers to contrast* situation of an action, is called the **Adverb of Concession or Compromise** (popularly known as **Negative Condition** for happening of an action).

They are introduced by the following sub-ordinate conjunctions; as, – *though, although, even, even if,* etc.
1) **Though** he is poor, he is honest.
2) **Even if** I fail, I shall not give up hope.
3) **Although** they were present, they were for nothing, they said nothing.
4) **Even** I had insulted you, you offered your help.

5) ***Even if*** none loves you, you should not hate them.

Note: Carefully note, *the adverb of Concession and the Adverb of Condition, have hardly any difference, or they are closely related.*

○ Adverbial clause of concession

Sometimes, adverbial clause of concession is introduced by <u>pronouns with an adverb 'ever'</u>; as, *whomever, whatever, however,* etc.
    1) ***However*** very strong you may be, I am not afraid of you.
    2) ***Whatever*** you may say, I don't believe you.
    3) ***Whoever*** he may be, he can't be allowed.
    4) ***Whoever*** you may be, I am not scared of you.
    5) ***Whatever*** you do, you'll sure fail in this examination.
    6) ***However,*** I helped her so many times, she admitted that never.
    7) ***However,*** I loved her, she merely hated through her life.

The adverb of Concession is almost like the adverb of Condition, already mentioned. However, carefully <u>note down the minute difference</u> in them.

Adverb of Condition or Supposition	Adverb of Concession or Compromise
1) ***If*** I succeed, I shall help you.	1) ***Though*** he is poor, he is honest.
2) I shall not go, ***unless*** you come.	2) ***Even if*** I fail, I shall not give up hope.
3) I may come in, ***in case*** I have time.	3) ***Although*** they were present, they were for nothing, they said nothing.
4) He will come, ***provided*** he gets leave.	4) ***However*** very strong you may be, I am not afraid of you.
5) I shall try, ***whether*** I succeed or not.	5) ***Whatever*** you may say, I don't believe you.

Points to remember: The minute difference lies in the fact that the adverb of condition, all do not express contrast but positive condition for an action, though contrast is it's a part. In case of concession or compromise, all express the contrast situation of an action.

(12)   **Adverb of Certainty**

The Adverbs of Certainty mostly like the Adverbs of Affirmation & Negation and they easily can be merged in. It <u>tells us of *'certainty of an action'* or *'the probability'*</u>.

The words that assure certainty or probability of an action are: *definitely, certainly, probably, perhaps*, etc.

1) **Certainly,** they will visit by tomorrow evening.
2) **Definitely** she will do or where will she go?
3) It will **probably** rain today by the evening.
4) **Perhaps** the train is late. It is half past ten, still no announce of its arrival at the station.

To be Noted: There are a group of adverbs we have, almost same in meaning & uses, or they are closely related, like-Time & Frequency, Place & Movement, Affirmation & Negation with Certainty & Focusing, Condition with the Compromise, Degree with the Manner, Time & Distance.

Ways, how Adverb of Certainty Modify Verbs. Follow the chart:

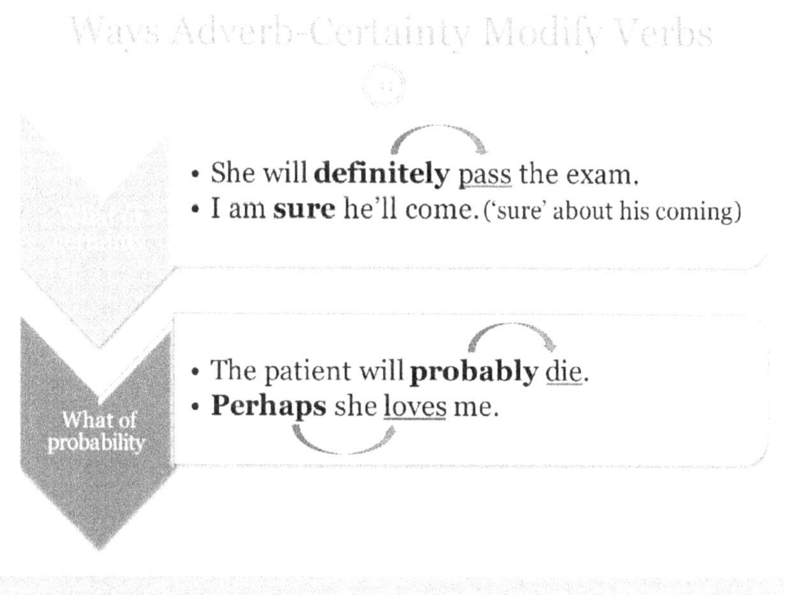

(13) **Focusing Adverb**

The adverbs <u>that point to</u> *one part of a clause/sentence*, i.e.

1) He has **even** gone to his enemy.
2) We are **only** going for two days.
3) The people present there were **mainly** politicians.

- This class of Adverb is used only to ***give focus on some particular part of a clause or sentence.***
- Like in the above, <u>in the *first sentence* the adverb *'even'* gives focus to the part of the sentence **'gone to his enemy'**,</u> and adds meaning to the verb 'gone'.
- In the 2nd sentence *the focus is centered on the duration of time,* '**only going for two days**.
- In the third sentence, the word '**mainly**' points to the <u>present number of people</u> who were 'politicians.

(14) Adverb of Degree or Quantity

Adverb of Degree or Quantity: The adverb or Adverb-phrases which show (answer to the questions) **'how much'**, **'in what degree'**, or **'to what extent'** something happens; as,
1) These mangoes are **_almost_** ripe. (Adds meaning to the adjective 'ripe'; <u>and thus, the following too</u>)
2) He was **_too_** careless.
3) The sea is **_very_** stormy.
4) I am **_rather_** busy.
5) I am **_fully_** prepared.
6) He is good **_enough_**.
7) I am **_so_** glad to see you again.
8) You are **_altogether_** mistaken.
9) Things are **_no_** better at present.
10) You are **_quite_** wrong.
11) She sings **_pretty_** well. (Adds meaning to another adverb)
12) He went/came **_nearer/further_**. (How far or near?)
13) I am **_partly_** right. He is **as** tall as Tom. (How much?)
14) I love her **little**. (How much?)
15) She believes me **enough**. (How much?)
16) We have done **a part of the project**. (To what extent?)
17) **Still,** we could not complete it. (To what extent?)
18) He is a genius **enormous**. (In what degree?)
19) I am **rather** a fool. (In what degree?)

Degrees or Forms of Comparison

○ Some adverbs, like adjectives, ***have three degrees (or forms) of comparison:*** *where the comparison is made* with none or nothing (zero comparison), namely '**Positive Degree**'; when it is between two, namely '**Comparative Degree**', & among more than two, namely the '**Superlative Degree**'; as,

- o He runs ***fast***. (Here: 'fast', the adverb form only modifying the verb 'run'; no comparison is made with anybody)
- o He runs ***faster*** *than* you. (Here: 'faster', besides modifying the verb 'run' hints the comparison which is made between 'he' & 'you'.)
- o He runs ***fastest of all*** in the race. (That means among all)

Note: In superlative, the article '**the**' is not essential like in the superlative degree of adjective ('the fastest runner').

❏ Mostly the Adverb of **Degree, Manner, Time** & **Position** has their Forms of Comparison; as, (far-further-furthest; near-nearer-nearest, etc.)

How to form Degrees or Forms of Comparison:

✖ If the adverb is of one syllable, we form the comparative by adding '**-er**' & the superlative by '**-est**' to the positive degree or form; as,
  - ▪ Fast—faster—fastest,
  - ▪ Hard—harder—hardest,
  - ▪ Long—longer—longest
  - ▪ Soon—sooner—soonest

✖ If the adverb ends in '**ly**', then add '**more**' & '**most**' before the adverb respectively in comparative & superlative Degree; as,
  - ▪ Skillfully—more skillfully—most skillfully
  - ▪ Swiftly—more swiftly—most swiftly

Except some; like,
  - ▪ 'Early'—earlier—earliest.

❏ It is noticed that mostly, though not only, the **Adverbs of Manner, Degree, Time & Position** admit of comparison; and many Adverbs, from their nature, cannot be compared; as, now, then, where, there, once—do not admit any comparison.

Study examples in the sentences:

a) Bhima shot his arrow *skillfully*.
- o   Yudhishthira shot his arrow ***more skillfully*** than Bhima.
- o   But, Arjuna shot his arrow ***most skillfully*** of all.

b) I did the job *swiftly*.
- o   You did the job ***more swiftly***.
- o   But, she did hers ***most swiftly*** of all of us there.

c) I came *early* this morning.
- o   You came ***earlier***.
- o   But, Shyamal came ***earliest*** of all.

d) Rama writes *well*.
- o   Arjun writes ***better*** than Rama.
- o   Narayan writes ***best*** of all.

e) Do you work *much*?
- o   I work ***more than*** you do.
- o   She works ***most*** of three of us. She is our mother.

❏ **To be noted:** Article 'the' is **not essential to be used with superlative adverb** in the sentence, though that is with the superlative adjective in the sentence; as,
- → He is the best student in the class. ('best' is the superlative adjective, preceding 'the' article.)
- → He runs worst of all. ('worst' is the superlative adverb, does not precede 'the' article in the sentence.)

✶ **Study the 'Degrees' or 'Forms of Comparisons' of Some Adverbs:**

Positive	Comparative	Superlative
Ill, badly	Worse	worst
Well	Better	Best
Much	More	Most
Little	Less	Least
(nigh)	Nearer	Nearest

Near

Far	Farther/further	Farthest/furthest
Late	Later	Latest
Loud	Louder	Loudest
Wisely	More wisely	Most wisely
Patiently	More patiently	Most patiently

Compare the <u>Degree of Adverbs</u> & the <u>Degree of Adjectives</u>

Degree of Adverbs	Degree of Adjectives
1. He <u>runs</u> **faster**.	1. He is a *fast* <u>runner</u>.
2. The work is **badly** <u>done</u>.	2. You are a **bad** <u>boy</u>.
3. It <u>worked</u> **worst**!	3. He was one of the ***worst*** <u>boys</u> in the class.
4. The leader <u>spoke</u> **loudly**.	4. Don't use ***loud*** <u>speaker</u> here.
5. It <u>worked</u> **better**.	5. He is a ***better*** <u>boy</u>.
6. **Wisely** they <u>performed</u> their tasks.	6. <u>They</u> were ***wise*** in their task.
7. They <u>went</u> **nearer** to the beach.	7. <u>You</u> are ***nearer*** to me.

Note: the above bold words are the superlative forms, while the underlined are the words they add meaning or qualify. In the first column they add meaning to the verb underlined. In the second column they bold words qualify the nouns or pronouns underlined.

Relative or <u>*Wh- Adjunctive*</u> & Interrogative Adverbs

(15)   **Relative Adverbs**

The adverbs ('wh' words) which like relative pronouns, ***relates or refers back to its antecedents & modifies as usual an adverb does*** to some words like verb, an adjective or another adverb or a phrase or a clause, are called the **Relative Adverbs**.

Relative adverbs like relative pronouns <u>join two parts of a sentence or two clauses</u>, and introduce Relative or Adjective clause in the sentence. Study the examples carefully:

1) **Tell them the reason <u>why</u> you came.**
   [You came for some purpose or for a reason. You tell them the reason.] After joining the independent sentences, the first one has turned to be '**why you came**', which is a relative clause, introduced by Relative Adverb '**why**'. 'why' denotes the reason.

2) **I know the street <u>where</u> the bank is.**
   [The bank is located somewhere at Gayeshwar Street. I know the street.] After joining the independent sentences, the first one has turned to be '**where the bank is**' which is a relative or adjective clause, introduced by Relative Adverb '**where**', which denotes 'place'.

3) **Show me the house <u>where</u> (=in which) he was assaulted.**
   [He was assaulted in a house. You know the house. You show me the house.] After joining the independent sentences, the first two sentences have turned to be one clause '**where (= in which) he was assaulted**' which is a relative clause, introduced by Relative Adverb '**where**', denotes 'place'.

4) **This is the reason <u>why</u> I left her.**
   [There was a reason. [May be, she boasts of too much. This is the reason.] For which I left her.] After joining the independent sentences, the first one, two or three sentences have turned to a condensed clause '**why I left her**' *(where one sentence is understood or implied)* and the clause is a relative clause, introduced by Relative Adverb '**why**', which denotes reason.

5) **Do you know the time <u>when</u> Gour Express comes?**
   [Gour Express comes at a certain time. I don't know the time. Do you know the time?] After joining the independent sentences, the first two sentences have turned to a condensed clause '**when Gour Express comes**' where one sense 'I don't know the time' remains understood or implied, and the clause is a relative clause, introduced by Relative Adverb '**when**', denoting time.

6) **I remember the house <u>where</u> I was born.**
   [I was born in a house. I remember the house.] After joining the independent sentences, the first one has turned to be '**where I was born**' which is a relative clause, introduced by Relative Adverb '**where**', denotes 'place'.

7) Tell me the direction, please; **where** is the Post Office?
[I don't know the way to the Post Office. Tell me the direction, please.] After joining the independent sentences, the first one has turned to be '*where is the post office*' which relates back to its antecedent noun 'direction'; so, the clause is a relative clause, introduced by a Relative Adverb '*where*'.

8) Tell me at least a reason **why** should I believe you?
[You want I should believe you. Tell me at least one reason.] After joining the independent sentences, the first one has turned to a clause '*why should I believe you*' which is a relative clause, introduced by Relative Adverb '*why*'.

9) Confess your crime **how** you committed.
[You committed a crime. In what way you did that. You must confess. /In what way you committed the crime. You must confess.] After joining the independent sentences, the first one or ones have turned to be '*how you committed*' which is a relative clause, relates back to its antecedent noun 'crime'. The clause is introduced by Relative Adverb '*how*'.

To be remembered: The **type of a clause depends upon the work done by it**, but not on linking words solely. Based on its work, role or function, a clause may be **a Noun, Adjective or Adverbial clause**. Read the chart. (For details, visit to the chapter of Clause.):

A sentence in different clauses:

The **type of a clause depends upon the work done by it**, but not on linking words. That's why a clause may be a **Noun/ Adjective /Adverbial** clause.		
	I know *where he lives*.	**Noun clause,** (object of 'know' by question —what do you know?)
	I know the place *where he lives*.	**Adjective clause,** (qualifying or describing the 'place' by question —which place?)
	I shall go *where he lives*.	**Adverbial clause,** (add meaning to the verb 'shall go'-by question —where? Where will you go?)

To be Noted: The **wh- relative adverbs**—where, why, when, how when preceding antecedent noun or pronoun, are often termed as **Relative Pronouns** by some grammarians, like 'Who', What' & Which' but it is confusing, for ***they [where, why, when & how]*** hardly used in place of any noun or a pronoun, like 'who', 'what', 'which' do.

To avoid this confusion, Peter suggests, you may put blame solely on him, to term these as 'Wh- Adjunctive Adverbs' rather than to say as **'Relative Adverbs'** or as **'Relative Pronouns',** as they do not only introduce relative or adjective clauses, but also Noun, or an Adverbial clause too, by their function or role in the sentence, like in the above chart. For the rest, however, you may try with written above.

(16)   Interrogative Adverb:

When adverbs ('wh.' words) are used ***in asking question***, they are called **Interrogative Adverbs**. The interesting thing is their <u>answers are always other Simple Adverbs</u>; as,

    a.   When, how, why, how many, how far, where etc. are the *wh. words which are used to ask questions to get Simple Adverbs*. Study the examples and read their answers what roles they do in the sentences.

1) **Where** is your Ram? (The answer is 'adv. of place' = in Heaven / at Ajodhya, etc.)
2) **When** will He come to save you from your difficulties? (The answer is adv. of time = after my salvation / when time will come, etc.)
3) **Why** are you late? (The answer is adv. of reason = Because I was with her in her bed / Because my spouse had not me fed / Because I woke up late, etc.)
4) **How** did you do it? (The answer is adv. of manner = patiently/in patience)
5) **How** much work can he do in a day? (The answer is adv. of degree = seven tones in a day, etc.)
6) **How** high is Kutub Minar? (The answer is adv. of degree, adds meaning to an adj. = 73 meters long. [Long/tall—are adjectives. 73 metre are adv. Of degree.])

In the above sentences, the bold **'wh' words** are the interrogative adverbs but <u>their answers are the simple adverbs, either they are in single words or in phrases.</u>

Compare-**Relative Adverb** & **Interrogative Adverb** in the following chart:

Relative Adverb	Interrogative Adverb
1) Tell her the reason <u>why</u> I love her.	1) <u>Why</u> do I love her?
2) I know the place <u>where</u> she lives.	2) <u>Where</u> does she live?
3) Tell me the time <u>when</u> you'll come, my love.	3) <u>When</u> will you come?
4) Tell the way <u>how</u> you succeeded.	4) <u>How</u> did you succeed?

Exercise-1:

A. In the following sentences, **(1) pick out the Adverbs & tell what each modifies; (2) tell whether the modified word is a Verb, an Adjective, or an Adverb, a phrase or a clause; & (3) classify the Adverb** (denote their class, as Adverb of Time, Place, Manner, Degree or other).

1.	Try again. He is too shy.	2.	We rose very early. I am so glad to hear it.
3.	Cut it lengthwise. Too many cooks spoil the broth.	4.	Are you quite sure? This is well said.
5.	Once or twice, we have met alone.	6.	The railway station is far off.
7.	I have heard this before.	8.	Father is somewhat better.
9.	I am much relieved to hear it.	10.	The walk was rather long.
11.	The patient is much worse today.	12.	Ambition urges me forward.
13.	She was dressed all in black.	14.	We were very kindly received.
15.	Her son is out in India.	16.	I surely expect him tomorrow.
17.	He could not speak; he was so angry.	18.	You are far too hasty.
19.	The secret is out.	20.	He is old enough to know better.
21.	I would much rather not go.	22.	You need not roar.
23.	He went off on Monday.	24.	Wisdom is too high for a fool.
25.	There is a screw loose somewhere.	26.	I see things differently now.

<table>
<tr><td>27. Rome was not built in a day.</td><td>28. The door burst open and in they came.</td></tr>
<tr><td>29. Do not crowd your work so closely together.</td><td>30. Do not walk so fast.</td></tr>
<tr><td>31. Order the carriage round.</td><td>32. He has been shamefully treated.</td></tr>
<tr><td>33. I wonder you never told me.</td><td>34. The snake stealthily vanished from our sight.</td></tr>
</table>

B. <u>Fill in the blanks with suitable Adverbs</u>

1) Tortoise walks _______ (Manner).
2) We will have our Semester exams on ________(Time).
3) The accident happened near the _______(Place).
4) At least _______ a week I used to go for Temple (Frequency).
5) We all go for a picnic just for ______ (Purpose).
6) The sea is very _______ (Degree /Quantity).
7) ______you are mistaken (Affirmation/Negation).

<u>Answers</u>

1) Tortoise walks <u>slowly</u> (Manner).
2) We will have our Semester exams on <u>April 1ˢᵗ week</u> (Time).
3) The accident happened near the <u>Highway</u> (Place).
4) At least <u>twice</u> a week I used to go for Temple (Frequency).
5) We all go for a picnic just for <u>enjoyment</u> (Purpose).
6) The sea is very <u>stormy</u> (Degree /Quantity).
7) <u>Surely</u> you are mistaken (Affirmation/Negation).

C. <u>Try this exercise with the adverbs supplied below:</u>

1) His face was dirty and he was dressed --------------------. (manner)
2) Have you--------------- --------------------- been in a plane? (frequency)
3) She was so ill that she missed school ----------------------. (duration)
4) I did some homework last night and finished it------------------. (time)
5) We went------------------------------- to play. (place)
6) Dad takes the dog for a walk ---------------------------. (frequency)
7) Sally left her pencil case---------------------------------. (Place)
8) Speak -------------------------so everyone can hear you. (manner)

9) It was a fine day and the children played in the garden ------.
   (duration)
10) "Go and do your homework." "I've--------------------done it."
   (time)

(Outside – this morning – ever – on the bus – clearly –all day
–in old clothes– for a week– already– every   day)

Answers:

1. His face was dirty and he was dressed **in old clothes**.
   (manner)
2. Have you **ever** been in a plane? (frequency)
3. She was so ill that she missed school **for a week** (duration)
4. I did some homework last night and finished it **this morning**.
   (time)
5. We went **outside** to play. (place)
6. Dad takes the dog for a walk **every day**. (frequency)
7. Sally left her pencil case **in the bus.** (place)
8. Speak **clearly** so everyone can hear you. (manner)
9. It was a fine day and the children played in the garden **all
   day**. (duration)
10. "Go and do your homework." "I've **already** done it." (time)

The Forms & Formation of Adverbs

When we are reading of forms of adverbs, it means, how adverbs look. Like any part of Speech, Adverbs too have multi forms. However, there are also a lot of which can be formed from others. Study the following points, regarding the forms and formation of Adverbs:

A. Different parts of speech, generally, take different forms. However, *some may have also corresponding forms but their uses & meanings are different; as,*

- o It is so **yesterday** fashion! (As an Adjective)
- o They arrived **yesterday**. (As an Adverb)

B. Some adverbs end in '-ly' but there are others which **do not have 'ly' ending**; as,

- o **Kindly** do the favor. (Adverb ends in '-ly')

o   Come **here**. (Adverb without '-ly' ending)

✘ The best way to identify a part of speech is to study the functions of certain part of speech and to know its difference from others. However, understanding of forms and formation help a learner quite a far.

✘ **Adverbs**, **Prepositions**, **Adjectives** as well as **Nouns** have lots of corresponding forms, but their uses, as said, are always different.

C. Corresponding forms of **Adjectives** & **Adverbs**. Study them carefully:

1. He spoke in a **loud** voice. (In the underlined phrase, '**loud**' is an adjective, as it describes its following noun 'voice'; but the entire phrase '**in a loud voice**' is an adverbial phrase, modifying the manner of the verb 'spoke'; how did he speak? = in a loud voice.)

2. He talks so **loud**. (He talks so **loudly**) (here in 'loud' & 'loudly'— both are adverbs, adds meaning to the verb, 'talk')

Note: Thus, identity or classification of words vastly depend on their uses in the sentence, but not merely on forms.

✘ Study more in the following chart:

Used as Adjectives	Used as Adverbs
1. Roshan is our **fast** bowler.	1. Roshan can bowl **fast**.
2. He lives in the **next** house.	2. When I **next** see him, I shall speak to him.
3. He went to the **back** entrance.	3. Go **back**.
4. Every **little** difficulty ruffles his temper.	4. He is **little** known outside India.
5. This is a **hard** sum.	5. He works **hard** all day.
6. It's an **ill** wind that blows nobody good.	6. I can **ill** afford to lose him.
7. He is the **best** boy in the class.	7. He behaves **best**.
8. He is **quick** to take offence.	8. Run **quick**.
9. Are you an **early** riser?	9. We started **early**.
10. The teacher has a **high** opinion of that boy.	10. Always aim **high**.

11. He is the **only** child of his parent.
12. We have food **enough** to last a week.
13. He is no **better** than a fool.
14. There is **much** truth in what he says.

11. You can **only** guess.
12. She sings well **enough**.
13. He knows me **better** than you.
14. The patient is **much** better.

D. <u>**Adverbs with double forms:**</u> There are some adverbs which have two forms, one <u>ends in 'ly'</u> & other <u>without 'ly'</u>. They may have same meaning; like, **'he sings very loud'** & **'he sings very loudly'**—both have same meanings.

✼ However, *most of adverb with double forms have different meanings*; as,

a) William works **hard** (=diligently).
b) I could **hardly** (scarcely) recognize him.

c) Stand **near** (opposed to distant).
d) They two are **nearly** (closely) related.

e) We arrived **late** (opposed to early).
f) I have not seen him **lately** (recently).

g) I am **pretty** (quite; fairly) sure of the fact.
h) She is **prettily** (neatly, elegantly) dressed.

E. The use of '**Adverbial Accusative**': Nouns or Adjectives denoting **adverbial** relations of time, place, distance, weight, measurement, value, degree or the like, are often used as adverbs — are known as '**Adverbial Accusative**.

[However, the term '**accusative**' refers to nouns, adjective or the forms of pronouns used in the direct object or connected with the direct object.]

Study in the following of adverbial accusative.

1) The program lasted a _week_. ('week' is a noun, refers 'the name of seven days' as a unit, but 'a week' is used in the sentence as **an adverbial phrase** *to denote 'time of adverb'*; as it adds meaning to the verb 'lasted'. 'How long did the program last for?')

2) He went ***home***. ('home' denoting 'place of adverb', adds meaning to the verb 'went'. Where did he go? When 'home' comes from a noun.)
3) The load weighs four ***tones***. (refers 'weight')
4) The cloth measures three ***meters***. (Refers measurement of 'length')
5) The wound was ***skin-deep***. (refers 'degree')
6) This will last me a ***month***.
7) We walked five ***miles***.
8) It measures five ***feet***.
9) The watch is only fifty ***rupees***.

('fifty rupees' refers 'value', the price of the watch, 'how much did you pay? /How much you paid?' Here, it may raise a confusion regarding 'The watch is costly'. 'Costly' is an adjective describing the noun, 'watch'; but 'The watch is only fifty rupees', 'fifty rupees' neither refers to the watch itself nor describing it as 'costly', but refers its value, its price, 'how much one pay for the watch. So, it is an adverb.)

The nouns used so, are known as '**Adverbial Accusative**'.

- However, there are some adverbs also may be used as **Nouns** & **Adjectives**:

- Some Adverbs are used as Nouns used after preposition; as,
  - He lives far from ***here*** (this place).
  - He comes from ***there*** (that place).
  - I have heard that before ***now*** (this time).
  - By ***then*** (that time) the police arrived on the scene.
  - Since ***when*** (what time) have you taken to smoking?
  - The rain comes from ***above*** (the sky).

- Certain Adverbs can be used also as Adjectives, when some participle is understood in the sentence; as,
  - The ***then*** king = the king then reigning.
  - A ***down*** train = a down-going train.
  - An ***up*** train = an up-going train.
  - The ***above*** statement = the statement made above.

Formation of Adverbs

A. Adverbs of Manner are mostly formed from Adjectives by adding '-**ly**'; as,

Beautiful—beautifully; clever—cleverly; wise—wisely;
foolish—foolishly; kind—kindly; quick—quickly;
Sad—sadly; sweet—sweetly; wonderful—wonderfully;

B. When adjective ends in '**y**' preceded by a consonant, *change '**y**' into '**i**', and then add '-**ly**';* as,

Happy—happily; heavy—heavily; ready-readily;

C. When the adjective ends in '**le**', simply *change '**e**' into '**y**' to form adverb*; as,

Double—**doubly**; single—**singly**, etc.

o   I am living here **singly**. No problem till now with the locals.
o   They did it **doubly** but the credit goes to the boss only.

❑ **Study the differences in Forms & Uses:**

Used as an Adjective	**Used as an Adverb**
1. John is a **kind** man.	1. John spoke to him **kindly**.
2. They were **happy** couple.	2. After that they lived **happily**.
3. It is a **beautiful** garden.	3. It was decorated **beautifully**.
4. The load was **heavy**.	4. He bounced **heavily** to crack it down.
5. She spent **single** life.	5. She lived life **singly**.
6. He led a **double** life.	6. **Doubly** we are incomparable.
7. It is so **yesterday** fashion.	7. They arrived **yesterday**.
8. The baby was sound **asleep** *(sleeping deeply, describing the baby. It's an adjective).*	8. He replied **asleep**. *(Adverb of manner; replied while he was sleeping)*

❑ **Note: '-ly' ending words are not only the adverbs:**

✖ The words *friendly, lively, kindly*, and *lonely* <u>are usually adjectives</u>. Study them in the following sentences:
   o   He is **friendly.**
   o   He is **lively.**
   o   He is **kindly.**
   o   He is **lonely.** (He feels lonely)

✘ In each sentence **the '–ly' words** are qualifying a person, 'he'. However, it may also describe things; as,
  - o She was wearing a **lovely** dress.
  - o It was a very **lively** party.

✘ <u>Though we have adverbs with **'ly'** ending</u>, there are larger than that number <u>have adverbs without **'-ly'**; as,</u>

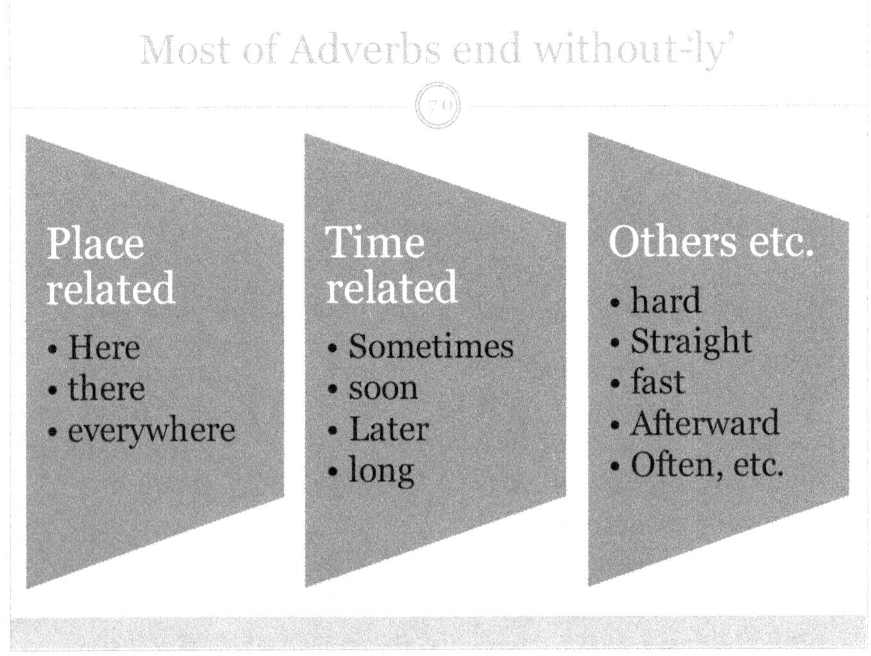

D. Some Adverbs are made up of a **Noun** & **qualifying Adjective**; as,

➤*Meantime, meanwhile, midway, otherwise, sometime, yesterday;*
1) I was thinking to go. **In the meantime**, he arrived.
2) I'll contact them soon. **Meantime** don't tell them I'm back.
3) The doctor will see you again next week. **Meanwhile**, you much rest as much as possible.

➤*Meantime = meanwhile= while something else is happening in the period of between two times or events)*
4) The hotel is situated **midway** between two stations.
5) The goal was scored **midway** through the first half.

➤*Midway= in the middle of a period of time; between two places.*
6) Shut the window, **otherwise** it'll get too cold in here.
7) My parents lent me the money. **Otherwise**, I couldn't have afforded the trip.

➤*Otherwise = used to state what the result would be, if sometimes did not happen or if the situation were different.*
8) **Sometimes**, I go by car. (=*occasionally rather than all the time*)
9) She **sometimes** writes to me. I like to be on my own sometimes.
10) Where were you **yesterday morning**? They arrived **yesterday**.
E. Some adverbs are compounds of a **preposition** like 'a' (weakened form of 'on') or 'be' (from middle English 'bi' ['by']), 'to', 'over' & a **noun**; as,
Abed (on bed), aboard (on board), afoot (on foot), ahead (on head), asleep (on sleep), away (on way); besides (by + sides), betimes, overboard, to-day, to-morrow (also: today & tomorrow), etc.

1) He was lying **abed** and cursing us for our deaths. What a man!
2) We went **aboard**. He was already **aboard** the plane.
3) The plane crashed, killing all 157 passengers **aboard**.
➤Aboard = on or onto a ship, plane, bus or train.
➤Afoot = being planned, happening; on foot
4) There are blue prints **afoot** to increase taxation.
5) Sometimes they come **afoot** (on foot).
➤Ahead = further forward in space or time; in front.
6) I'll run **ahead** and warn them. The road **ahead** was blocked.
7) We've got a lot of hard work **ahead**.
8) He replied **asleep**. (Adverb of manner; replied while he was sleeping)
9) The baby was sound asleep (sleeping deeply, describing the baby. It's an adjective).
10) The beach is a mile **away**. (= to or at a distance from somebody or something)
11) Christmas is still a month's **away**.
12) I don't really want to go. **Besides,** it's **too** late now.
➤Besides = used for making an extra comment that adds to what you have just said.
➤Betimes =in a good season of time; early, especially in the morning. / In a short time or soon)
13) I'll try my best to finish it **betimes**.

F. Some are compounds of a **preposition**& an **adjective**; as, (along, aloud, anew, behind, below, beyond, etc.)
1) I was **just** walking **along** singing myself

2) We're going for a swim. Why don't you come **along**?
3) The book is coming **along nicely**.
4) Along= forward with somebody, towards a better state or position, etc.
5) Aloud= in a voice that other people can hear/ in a loud voice
6) He read the letter **aloud** to us. She cried **aloud** in protest.
7) What am I going to do? She wondered **aloud**.
8) Anew = to do something in a different way.
9) They started a life **anew** in Canada.
10) Sit **beside** me. He is **behind** us.
11) The rabbit is **under** the tree. It is **beyond** our reach.

G. Many a preposition are used to form adverbial phrase; as, (In, out, on, up, above, below, over, within, without, before, beneath, etc.) Now study them in the sentences to understand the difference better.
1) He is shouting **_from the top_**.
2) We are learning **_in class-room_**.
3) She is sitting **_under a tree_**.
4) Two other guards stood **_behind him_**.
5) We were walking **_along the road_**.
6) They were walking **_on the treadmill_**.
7) All of us sat **_in awkward silence for a few seconds_**.
8) The maid skipped her work **_two days in a row_**.
9) Who were grazing **_in the field_**?
10) Stand you all **_in a line_**.

H. Study the chart of adverb which are said to come from pronouns— the(that), he (here), who ('wh'):

Pronouns	Place	Motion to	Motion from	Time	Manner
That	There (that place)	Thither (to or towards that place)	Thence (from that place)	Then (that time)	Thus (that way)
this	Here (this place)	Hither (to this place)	Hence (from here/from this place; after a length of time in	--	--

the future;
for this
reason)

wh	Where (what place)	Whither (where or to which place; what is likely to happen to something in the future)	Whence (from where)	When (at what time)	How (in what manner)

How to use them in the sentences

1) He is coming **hither** (to this place).
2) **Hither** he is coming, everyone be alert.
3) **Thither** (to/towards that place) she is going, keep watch on her.
4) People began rushing **hither & thither**. (Also, hither & yon)
5) *Whither* = where/ to which place; used to ask what is likely to happen to something in the future.
6) **Whither** should they go? They did not know **whither** they should go.
7) **Whither** modern architecture after this decade?
8) **Whither** modern technology, let us know in the seminar.
9) We have belief in his abilities. **Hence** (for this reason), we must motivate the child.
10) We suspect she is hiding something; **hence** it needs an impartial enquiry.
11) They made their way from Spain to France &**thence** (from that place) to England.
12) He was promoted to manager, **thence** to a partnership in the farm.
13) The aliens returned **whence** (from where) they had come.
14) Many scholars have argued **thus** (in this way/like this).
15) The university has expanded colleges, **thus** allowing more students the chance of higher education. Don't come **here** (this placc) so frequently. Don't go **there** (that place) **ever**.
16) **Where** (what place) have you been **yesterday**?

I. Many adverbs are compounded with Prepositions (i.e., they are formed by 'adverb+ preposition'); as,

- **'here' + prep** = Hereabouts, hereafter, hereby, herein, hereof, hereto, heretofore, hereupon, herewith,
- **'there' + prep** = Thereabouts, thereafter, thereby, therefore, therefrom, therein, thereof, thereon, thereto, thereunder, thereupon, therewith,
- **'hither'/ 'hence'/ 'thence' + prep** = hitherto, henceforth, henceforward, thenceforth, thenceforward, etc.
- **'where' + prep** = whereabouts, whereby, wherever, wherefore, wherein, whereon, whereupon, etc.
- Besides using as adverb, some of the above, and others as _whereas_, _whereof_, are used as Conjunctions.

Using them in the sentences

1) There aren't many houses **hereabouts** (also: hereabout, near this place).
2) Here is not found your name on this page & **hereafter** (in the rest of the document).
3) **Hereafter** (also: 'hereinafter', from this time) you are not my friend.
4) **Hereby** it is admitted, most sorrowfully, she is no more with us.
5) **Hereby**, it is declared we have no objection with Mr. Sarkar if he gets a better chance. (Legally declared something/as a result of this statement)
6) He is not **herein** (in this place) since the last year.
7) **Herein** (in the document/statement) I have not found any discrepancy.
8) Neither party is willing to compromise and **herein** lies the problem.
9) I'll not take a part **hereof** (of this), as I donated her all.
10) Please see the policy **hereto** (to this) appended.
11) She never behaved so **heretofore** (before this time).
12) She insulted me. I haven't visited **hereupon** (after this, as a direct result of this situation). She didn't come **hereupon** as I have insulted her once.
13) I enclose **herewith** (with this letter, book or document) a copy of my Aadhar card for verification.
14) Please, enclose **herewith** a copy of your policy.

15) Peter is from Balurghat or ***thereabouts*** in Wet Bengal. (Near the place mentioned)
16) They paid ten million rupees or ***thereabouts*** for the piece of land. (Near about the particular number, quantity, time or age, mentioned, which is not exact)
17) She must be 18 or ***thereabouts*** by then.
18) She married at 17 & gave birth to her first child shortly ***thereafter*** (after the time or event), swallowed her career and dream!
19) Regular exercise strengthens the heart, ***thereby*** (as the result of an action or situation, mentioned) reducing the risk of heart attack.
20) He is only 17 and ***therefore*** (due to that reason, logical) not eligible to cast vote.
21) There is still much to discuss. We shall, ***therefore***, return to this topic at our next meeting.
22) The committee will examine the agreement & any problem arising ***therefrom*** (from the thing mentioned).
23) The insurance policy covers the building and any fixture contained ***therein*** (in the document, place or object, mentioned).
24) In court she denied any knowledge of the article and the allegations made ***therein***.
25) Is the property or any part ***thereof*** (of the thing mentioned) used for commercial activity?
26) A meeting to discuss the annual accounts & the auditor's report ***thereon*** (on the thing, mentioned).
27) The lease entitles the holder to use the buildings and any land attached ***thereto*** (to the thing mentioned).
28) This savings plan is only available under the Finance Act 1990 & any regulations made ***thereunder*** (under the thing, mentioned).
29) The audience ***thereupon*** (immediately after the situation) rose cheering to their feet.
30) A large notice with black letters printed ***thereupon***.
31) ***Therewith*** (with the thing already mentioned /soon after) I like to give 'thanks' for all you have done for me.
32) Friday, 31 July 1925 ***henceforth*** (also: 'henceforward', from this particular time and all the times in the future) became known as Red Friday.
33) Thursday, 25 Dec. 2019 ***henceforward*** became known as 'Covid Day'.
34) ***Thenceforth*** (starting from that time) he became known as the lord of protector.
35) Her life ***hitherto*** (until now, until the particular time) had been devoid of adventure.
36) In my last visit to Sundarbans, I discovered a ***hitherto*** unknown

species of moth.

37) ***Whereabouts*** did you find it? (Used to ask general area where somebody, something is)
38) They have introduced a new system ***whereby*** all employees must undergo regular trainings.
39) ***Wherever*** (where) can he have gone to? (Used to ask expressing surprise to mean 'where')
40) ***Wherefore***, art thou Romeo? (What for/why/because of what)
41) It is an organization ***wherein*** (in which place, situation, condition or thing) each employee I valued & respected.
42) ***Wherein*** lies the difference between Feminism & Monism?
43) I love the ground ***whereon*** (on which/on what/where) he stands.
44) He told her, she was a liar, ***whereupon*** (as a result of this) she walked out.

J.   Sometimes, two adverbs go together, joined by conjunction 'and'; as,

a.   **Again & again** = more than once, repeatedly;
b.   **By and by** = before long; presently; after a time;
c.   **Far & away** = decidedly; beyond all comparisons; by a great deal;
d.   **Far & near** = in all directions;
e.   **Far & wide** = comprehensively;
f.   **First & foremost** = first of all;
g.   **Now & again** = at intervals; sometimes; occasionally;
h.   **Now & then** = from time to time; occasionally;
i.   **Off & on** = not regularly; not intermittently;
j.   **Once & again** = on more than one occasion; repeatedly;
k.   **Out & away** = beyond comparison; by far;
l.   **Out & out** = decidedly; beyond all comparison;
m.   **Over & above** = in addition to; besides; as well as;
n.   **Over & over** = many times; frequently; repeatedly;
o.   **Through & through** = thoroughly & completely;
p.   **Thus & thus** = in such & such a way;
q.   **To & fro** = backwards & forwards; up & down

Using them in the sentences

1)   Good book should be read *again and again*.
2)   I warned him *again & again* not do that.
3)   *By and by* the tumult will subside.
4)   *By and by* he became a renowned writer.
5)   Her fame has spread *far & near*.
6)   As a statesman he saw *far & wide*.
7)   This is *far and away* the best course.

8) He is _far and away_ the best bowler in our eleven.
9) He _now and then_ writes on fiscal questions.
10) I write to him _now and then_.
11) He worked five years, _off & on_, on 'Peter's Complete English Grammar'
12) I have told you _once and again_ that you must not read such trash.
13) This is _out and away_ the work on philosophy.
14) He gained _over and above_ this, the goodwill of all people.
15) _Over & above_ being hard-working he is thoroughly honest.
16) He reads all the novels of Paul _over & over_.
17) I believe he is _out and out_ the best Indian batsman.
18) He has read Milton _through & through_.
19) _Thus, and thus_ only we shall succeed.
20) He walked _to & fro_, meditating. He walked _to & fro_ doing nothing.

The Position of Adverbs

The place or position of an adverb in a sentence can be defined in the following ways:

Adverb of **Manner**, adverb or adverbial phrase of **Place, Time**— are generally placed after the verb or an object, if any, & if there is only one adverb; as,

1) It is raining **heavily**.
2) The ship is going **slowly**.
3) She speaks English **well**.
4) He does his work **carefully**.
5) He will come **here**.
6) I looked **everywhere**.
7) Hang the picture **there**.
8) I met him **yesterday**.
9) They are to be married **next week**.

When there are two or more adverbs and they are to be used after verb or an object, the normal order of adverbs is: adverb of **Manner > Place & >Time**; as,

1) She sang _well **in the concert**_ in _last year_.
2) We should go _there **tomorrow evening**_.
3) He spoke _earnestly **at the meeting**_ _last night_.
4) All of us sat **_in awkward silence_** in _the meeting hall_ **_for a few seconds_**.
5) Inspector Rana **_awkwardly_** put his cup **_down on_**

the table.

1) I am **never** *late* for my school.
2) He is **always** *at home* on Sundays.
3) We are **just** *off*. He is a **rather** *lazy* boy
4) I worked **only** *two* sums. She has slept **only** *three* hours.
5) The dog was **quite** *dead*.
6) The book is **very** *interesting*.
7) Do not speak **so** *fast*.
8) I have read **all** *through the book*.
9) **Suddenly**, *he arrived there*.
10) His wife **never** *cooks*.
11) He has **never** *seen* a tiger.
12) I have **often** *told* him to write neatly.
13) We **usually** *have breakfast* at eight.
14) My uncle has **just** *gone out*.
15) I **quite** *agree with* you.
16) He was **almost** *dead*. **Hardly** *has he done his work in time*.
17) He reached the party before **nearly** *three hours*.

1) Amal has come late again. Yes, he **always** does come *late*.
2) When will you write the essay? But I **already** have *written* it.
3) Will you be free on Sundays? I **usually** am *free* on Sundays.
4) Do you eat meat? Yes, I **sometimes** do. (do = eat meat)
5) I **often** have to *go* to college on foot.
6) He **always** used to *agree* with me.
7) I **only** worked *two* sums.
8) He has **only** slept *three* hours.

1) Is the box **enoug**h? (here 'enough' modifies the number of box or its' size, understood; i.e., modifying the adjective, not the noun 'box')
2) He has *rash* **enough** to interrupt.
3) He spoke *loud* **enough** to be heard.

4)   Amal has _come_ **late**.

❏ **Note:** we noticed that though adverbs generally used before the words it modifies, but they are also used after verb and object in the examples of Manner, Place & Time.
❏ When they are stressed, adverbs are shifted, and with certain adverbs like 'enough' adverb is used after the 'word' it modifies.
❏ Thus, _adverbs, based on its nature, may be used at anywhere in the sentences, at the beginning, center (like between subject & verb) and also at the end_.

Exercise-1: Insert the adverbs (or adverb phrases) in their normal position:
1)   He invited me to visit him (often).
2)   I am determined to yield this point (never).
3)   I know the answer (already).
4)   We have seen her (just, in the squire).
5)   I have to reach the office (by 9.30, usually)
6)   Will he be (there, still)?
7)   I shall meet you (this evening, in the park).
8)   The train has left (just).
9)   Can you park your car near the shop? Yes, I can (usually).
10) You have to check your oil before starting (always).
11) He is in time for meals (never).
12) We should come (here, one morning).
13) He has recovered from his illness (quite).
14) He goes to the cinema (seldom).
15) That is not good (enough).
16) You must say such a thing (never, again).
17) Suresh arrives (always, at 9 o'clock, at the office).
18) He played the violin (last night, brilliantly, in the concert).

2. Prepositions, Kinds & Uses

The chapter includes-
* Definition,

- <u>Kinds of Prepositions,</u>
  - Prepositional phrase,
- <u>The Functions of Prepositions,</u>
  - Special attention to some prepositions,
- <u>The Place of Prepositions,</u>
  - When they are used at the end.
- <u>Prepositional Objects or Complement.</u>
- Conjugation of Preposition with Nouns, Adjectives or Participle & Verbs (i.e., Certain Nouns, Adjective or Participle & Verbs take some particular Prepositions).

- **Read:**
  - → There is a cow *in* the field.
  - → He is fond *of* tea.
  - → The cat jumped *off* the chair.

- *In sentence 1,* the word '*in*' is placed before '*the field*' (mainly 'field'; 'the' is an article to define 'field') & *shows relation between two words, '**cow**' & '**field**' (both are Nouns).*

- *In sentence 2,* the word '*of*' is placed before '*tea*' & *shows relation between two words, '**fond**' & '**tea**' (Adj.& Noun).*

- *In sentence 3,* the word '*off*' is placed before '*the chair*' (mainly 'chair') & thus *shows relation between the two words, '**jumped**' & '**chair**' (Verb & Noun).*

- **Note:** Thus, **Prepositions generally used before Nouns** and they **show relation with** other words that may be **another Noun, an Adjective or a Verb,** like the above.
  - Here, the words— *in, of, off* —are the examples of Prepositions.

- **Definition: -**<u>Preposition is a word</u>, which is <u>generally used before a noun, noun phrase or a pronoun</u>, connecting it with another word in the sentence [that may be <u>another Noun, an Adjective or a Verb]</u> that shows relation between them.

<u>Study the following examples.</u>

He is swimming *in* the evening. ('**in**' is used before 'evening', and shows its relation with 'swimming', a *noun with a verb*. Here 'in' is the preposition. However, the phrase '**in the evening**' is an adverbial phrase, denoting '**time**' of the action 'swimming'.)

- We were looking ***towards*** the sky. ('looking' & 'sky', the verb and the noun— are shown related by the word 'towards' which is a preposition. However, the phrase 'towards the sky' denotes the adverb of movement.)

When Prepositions, used with Adjectives:
- Prepositions are often used with some adjectives, preceding them. The adjectives in these examples are underlined.
    - → Dad was angry ***with*** us.
    - → We were afraid ***of*** the big dog.
    - → She's not very interested ***in*** sports.
    - → John is very good ***at*** drawing.
    - → Mr. Lee is pleased ***with*** our work.
    - → The teachers are always kind ***to*** us.
    - → What's wrong ***with*** the computer?

When Prepositions, used with Verbs:
- Prepositions more frequently follow the verbs; like the followings *(The verbs in these examples are underlined and in color)*:
    - → I'm looking ***for*** my pencil. Have you seen it?
    - → Can you think ***of*** another word for 'pleased'?
    - → Does this book belong ***to*** you?
    - → We're listening ***to*** CDs.
    - → I agree ***with*** you, regarding this issue.
    - → Tell me ***about*** the show you saw.
    - → Cut the cake ***into*** five pieces.
    - → They borrowed money ***from*** the bank.
    - → The girl boasts ***of*** her out beauty.
    - → They laughed ***at*** us & we bore the humiliation.
    - → The principal sends ***for*** Kakuli madam for our help. (Ask somebody to come)

When Prepositions, used with Nouns:
- Prepositions are also used with nouns, preceding them like verbs & adjectives in the previous examples. The nouns in these examples are written in color and underlined.
    - → What's the answer ***to*** this question?
    - → Is there a reason ***for*** this delay?
    - → What's the matter ***with*** you?

→   Here's an *example* **of** good behavior.
→   *Congratulations* **on** winning the competition!
→   Traffic can cause *damage* **to** the environment.

○ **Exercise-1: Fill** *in the blanks with suitable prepositions <u>that</u> <u>denote</u> 'the functions of adverbs', written within the bracket:*
a) A cat was sitting __________the roof of my car. (place)
b) Some people were talking ____the movie. (time)
c) A man was coming_____ us on his bike. (direction)
d) The party starts_______ six o'clock. (time)
e) She put the book _____her bag. (place)
f) We walked_____ the street to the park. (place)
g) She keeps her slippers_____ her bed. (place)
h) We always wash our hands _____meals. (time)
i) She ran _____the house because she was frightened.   (direction)

○ **Exercise-2:** *Find out the relation the preposition made between:*

a) He kept the **pen in** the **bag**. (pen & bag, by preposition 'in'; shows 'place'.)
b) She wants money to become one of the rich **in** her town. (rich & town, between two Nouns)
c) I *listened* **to** you attentively. (listened & you, verb-pronoun)
d) The patient *wants* to be cure **before** her board examination. (between 'cure' & 'board examination')
e) We had *started* **by** then. (started & then, verb &adverb)
f) He was *surprised* **at** her saying this. (Between verb & -ing clause)
g) He was *surprised* **at what he said**. (verb & wh- clause)
h) He *wants* to go **in** the cinema hall. (go & cinema hall, verb & noun.)
i) Give *alms* **to** beggar. (Between two nouns)

Kinds of Prepositions

○ <u>According to form or structure</u>, Prepositions may be arranged in six types or classes—
        (1) Simple,
        (2) Double,
        (3) Compound,
        (4) Prepositional Phrase,
        (5) Participial Prepositions &

(6) Disguised Prepositions.

> Read them now in details-

(1) **Simple Prepositions:** Prepositions which consist of only one word. They are mostly of single syllable & some of two; as, *at, by, for, from, in, on, of, off, out, round, through, till, to, under, up, with,* etc.

    1) I place my book **on** the table.
    2) I saw a girl **in** the garden.
    3) The dry leaves fall **from** the trees.
    4) The boys are sitting **under** a tree
    5) Girl is sitting **on** the table.
    6) We shall have a Transparency Integrity seminar **in August** (*time*)
    7) The visitors are walking **round** the school(*direction*)
    8) Our principal will travel **by** train(*method*)
    9) Tima is walking **towards** the borehole.
    10) The boy was seen going **through** the fence.
    11) There is a cow **in** the field.
    12) He is fond **of** tea.
    13) The cat jumped **off** the chair.

(2) **Double Prepositions:** The Prepositions which are formed <u>by adding two simple prepositions, joined together or placed side by side</u>. Such prepositions are used when a single preposition does not express the sense properly; as, *away from, from among, from under, from within, into, onto, out of, throughout, unto, upon, within, without,* etc.

    1) The mouse ran **into** the room.
    2) Grace threw the ball **into** the bucket.
    3) She overturned the burning candle **onto** the table.
    4) One should be chosen **from among** the rest of candidates.
    5) The mouse peeps **from under** the table.
    6) A man in ragged cloths comes **from within** the house.

(3) **Compound Prepositions:** The Prepositions which are generally formed by prefixing *a shortened form of a simple preposition (like* in place of **'on'**, in place of **'by'**, or '<u>to any changed form</u>' of a simple preposition*)* with a *Noun, Adjective,* or an *Adverb*; as,

1) *about (on + bout),*	11) *behind* **(by+hind),**
2) *a<u>b</u><u>ove</u> (on+**by**+<u>up</u>),*	12) *below* **(by+low),**

3) *across (on + cross),*	13) *beneath (by+neath),*
4) *against (on + gain)*	14) *beside (by+side),*
5) *along (on+long),*	15) *between (by+twain),*
6) *amidst (on+ middle),*	16) *beyond (by+yonder),*
7) *among (on+**gemong**, meaning 'mingling'),*	17) *but (by+**out**, meaning except),*
8) *amongst,*	18) *inside (in+side),*
9) *around (on+round),*	19) *outside (out+side),*
10) *before (by+fore),*	20) *underneath (under+neath),* etc.

1) Jeremy is **behind** the chair.
2) Who is lying **underneath** the tree?
3) **Beyond** there you can see daffodils thousands in number.

Note: Practically, we don't need study these forms (how do they form) but study their uses; however, study of formation always helps to understand its meaning implied or explicit.

Prepositional Phrase

(4) **Complex or Phrase Prepositions:** The Prepositions which are formed by two or more words, with the force of a single preposition at the end; as, *according to, as for, because of, due to, owing to,* etc. and their meanings need to study differently other than the meaning of a simple preposition; as,

1) Act **according to** my instructions.
2) Why don't you come **along with** us?
3) **Agreeably to** the terms of the settlement, I herewith enclose a demand draft for Rs. 20000.
4) He could not attend the classes **because of** his illness.
5) **By reason of** his perverse attitude, he estranged his best friends.
6) **In consequence of** his illness, he could not finish the work in time.
7) **In event of** his dying heirless, his nephew would inherit the whole property.
8) There is an open field **in front of** our house.
9) Tom was standing **in front of her** house five hours.
10) You have come **from outside**.

11) He got the flat **in lieu of** all his sundry.
12) I took Arts **in place of** science.
13) **In spite of** hard labor, he could not succeed.
14) Mrs. Gosh joined the meeting **instead of** her husband.
15) He went there **instead of** me.
16) **Owing to** excessive rain, the flood occurs this year.
17) Rs 75,000 **in full settlement of** all your claims is up-to-date.
18) Whatever he does, he does **with an eye to** the main chance.

* **Exception:** Some phrases do not take any simple preposition at end; as, *'on this side'*, *'on board'*, etc.
  - **On this side** you can see the stretched green land.
  - **On board**, she recalled her boyfriend & rushed towards the door.

To be noted: On this side—is better to call an adverbial phrase, and 'on board'—is an adjective phrase, used as participle to qualify a noun or a pronoun, here a pronoun 'she'. However, remember: most of prepositional phrases or prepositions have an adverbial sense in their uses, besides they show relation between words. And some are used as participial too (as an adjective), to describe a noun or a pronoun.

Here is **the list of Complex Preposition** or **Prepositional Phrase**. Study them carefully:

Prepositional Phrases	Meaning...	Examples
At home in	Familiar with/skilled in	He is quite at home in Mathematics.
At the top of	Highest point	The man began to cry at the top of his cry.
Because of	Due to reason	She could not sing because of cough & cold.
By dint of	With help	By dint of hard work, he succeeded.
By force of	By power of	Even a difficult thing is made easy by force of habit.
By means of	Way of/virtue of	He won the honor by means of selfless service.
By the side of	Beside	A small river flows by the side of the small village.

By virtue of	With help	She stood first by virtue of hard labor.
For the sake of	For/cause	Netaji sacrificed his life for the sake of his country.
For want of	Due to lack of	The drought occurs for want of rain.
In accordance with	accordingly,	Your action is not in accordance with your word.
In connection with	Relating	In connection with your query, I am writing this letter.
In case of	If happen (something)	In case of his death his son will get the benefit.
In common with	Agree with	You should also be favored with the others.
In course of	During the time	In course of conversation, he also mentioned it.
In consideration of	Considering	In consideration of his hard work, he may succeed.
In defense of	In support of	The pleader made a good proceeding in defense of his client.
In favor of	In support of	The students spoke in support of their teacher.
In front of	Before/at front	They saw a hut in front of the palace.
In keeping with	Accordance with	His interest in religion is in keeping with his age.
In lieu of	Instead of/in place of	Please take my subscription in lieu of her.
In opposition to	On contrary of	Your view is in opposition to mine.
In order to	For/ due to	In order to get a good result, he studied very hard.
In quest of	For seek of	He went to the town in quest of any job.
In regard to	Regarding/about	I have nothing to say in regard to this matter.

In reply/ response to	Giving reply	In response to your advertisement, I am writing this one.
In respect of	Regarding	In respect of service, he is senior to me.
In spite of	Even of	In spite of his poverty, he refused help.
In support of	In support of	The students spoke in support of their teacher.
In the teeth of	Against	In the teeth of strong opposition, the bill was passed.
In view of	On considering	In view of the importance, I'll take prime carefulness.
On account of	Because of/due to	On account of his illness, he failed in the Exam.
On behalf of	For (somebody)	On behalf of me kindly give it to my wife.
On the brink of	At the point of	Bengal was on the brink of a terrible famine in 1942.
On the eve of	At the moment of	He made a great confusion on the eve of the occasion.
On the point of	At the moment of	She was on the point of bursting into tears.
With a view to	For purpose of	He went to Delhi with a view to taking part...
With reference to	Referring/mentioning	With reference to your letter, I have the honor to inform you.

✖ Some words with different prepositions used in different situations.

1st uses	Referring	2nd uses	Referring	3rd uses	Referring
Agree with	a person	Agree on	(a point)	Agree to	(a proposal)
Apply to	a person	Apply for	(the post)		
Angry with	a person	Angry for	something	Angry at	(conduct)
Appeal to	a person	Appeal for	something	Appeal against	(a wrong)

Blind in	(one eye)	Blind to	(a fault)		
Die of	(a disease)	Die from	(an effect)	Die for	(a cause)
Heir of	a person	Heir to	a property		
Live on	(food)	Live by	(a way)		
Pleased with	a person	Pleased at	something		
Quarrel with	a person	Quarrel for/ over/about	something		
Think of/ about	a person	Think over	something		

(5) **Participial Prepositions:** When a participle (present or past) is being used as a preposition in a sentence, & show relation with the subject or main verb of the main clause, it is distinguished as Participial Preposition; as, during, notwithstanding, preventing, being, except (being excepted), past (which is passed), having, considering, regarding, owing, etc.

1) *Barring (= except, apart from)* accident, the mail will arrive tomorrow.
2) *Concerning (=about)* yesterday's fire, there are many rumors in the bazaar.
3) *Considering (=on consideration)* your age, you have done a great thing.
4) Fresh fruit is available *during (=through the time of)* the winter.
5) All the boys passed *except (=but)* one. There was lot of *but* none.
6) *Notwithstanding (=in spite of)* his frown, his son went for an adventure to the jungle. I started reading at the hour *past (=after)* sunset.
7) *Pending (=until)* further orders, Mr. Ghosh will act as Headmaster.
8) I know nothing more *regarding (=in regard of / about)* this matter.
9) *Respecting* the plan you mention, I shall write to you hereafter.
10) *Touching (=with regard to)* this matter, I have not as yet made up my mind.

(6) **Disguised Prepositions:** These Prepositions are so called as outwardly they do not look like Prepositions, but actually they are derived from some Prepositions; as, 'a' from '**on**'; 'o' from '**of**'; 'be' from '**by**'. (**Compare:** Compound Prepositions). Read the examples:

1) The journey costs at three miles *a* rupee.
2) The garbage carrier van visits the locality once *a* week.
3) The ship came *a*shore.
4) It's five *o*' clock now.

Functions of Preposition

Functions of Prepositions:

A. Prepositions are *mostly adverb in nature*. In many cases they form adverbial phrases with nouns; as,
   - o 'In the evening' (adv. of time),
   - o 'Towards the sky' (adv. of direction),
   - o 'In the class-room', etc. (adverb of place)

B. Preposition 'to' is *used to form Infinitive Verb*; as,
   - o He is thinking ***to*** go there.
   - o He went market ***to*** buy a book.
   - o I took Peter's English Grammar to read.

C. A lot of prepositions are *used to form phrasal verbs*; as,
   - o He ***laughs at*** us. He ***sends for*** Bhima.
   - o He is ***searching for*** the note.
   - o He ***aims at*** to be a doctor.
   - o He ***boasted of*** his accomplishments.

D. Preposition '*of*' is used to *show possession or parts of* & '*by*' is used to *show the agent of an action*; as,
   - o We were charmed ***by*** the beauty ***of*** nature.
   - o The book is designed by Mr. Peter and who is also Mr. P.

The Adverbial Functions of Prepositions

There are a lot of prepositions which have adverbial functions, i.e., they are used to form Adverbs. They do functions of an adverb in the sentences. Carefully study the examples. Before so, study the following chart:

Place, Position	Time	Movement	Direction	Agent/Instrument, Manner	Cause / Reason	Contrast/Concession, etc.
At, about	At, In	Through	To	By	For	Of
Above, under, up	On, By	Across	Towards	With	From	About
On, In	before	Along	From	For	Of	Without
By, over, below	After, till/until	Up, down, onto, into,	Into	In	With	Out of
Between	During	Downward	At	From	Because of,	
Among	For, past	Off	In	Without	Due to	
After	From	Away from	around	Throughout	As for	
Beside	Since	Upward				
Down	Within	up to				

1. **Prepositions, denoting *Place*:**
   Preposition often with Nouns or adjective form a phrase which denote place of adverb, where something happens or exits; as,

a) Saini was sitting **_under_** a tree.
b) Lay **_under_** the table.
c) I leaned **_against_** the wall.
d) Don't sit **_beside_** me.
e) There's a wooden floor **_underneath_** the carpet.
f) He fell **_among_** the thieves and lost his all.
g) Some geese flew **_over_** their house.
h) She lies **_upon_** bed.
i) They quarreled **_among_** themselves.
j) John and Sarah were hiding **_inside_** the wardrobe.
k) He was **_at_** death's door. The cliff hangs **_over_** the sea.
l) There was a tree **_beside_** the river.
m) Balurghat is **_on_** Atreyee.
n) Sit **_on_** deck. Stood **_before_** the door.
o) We live **_within_** the house.
p) She hides **_behind_** the curtain.
q) It was **_below_** the surface.
r) I have a friend who lives **_in_** America.

Prepositions *of Place*

	Pointing	Examples
At	Less known village/ town/ a small region	We live at Balurghat.
In	Large town/district/country/a large region	We are residing in West Bengal.
On	Position touching surface/supported by/attached to	The book is on the table.
By	Nearness	I always sit by my window.
Between	In the middle of two things or objects	It fell between the two houses.
Among	In the centre of more than two objects	The plane crashed among the trees.
Above	Very up in the sky without touching surface	The sun shines above our head.
Over	Up in the sky without touching the surface.	The shirt is hanging over the table.

2. Prepositions, denoting *Time*:

❑ Some prepositions with other parts of speech form phrase that show when something happens. They are known as adverbial phrase, denoting time.

❑ Examples: -

School starts **_at_** nine o'clock.
_At_ 3 pm is your online class.
We're going to the zoo **_on_** Saturday.
_In_ the morning everyday she does exercise.
It's **_past_** your bedtime already.
I visited my grandparents **_during_** the summer.
You must finish the work **_by_** Friday.
I'll do my homework **_before_** dinner.

❑ Prepositions *of Time*

Prepositions *of Time*

	Pointing	Examples
In/on	In to mean a duration; on to mean specific day	It happened in the month of June. In Summer season, the building completed. In 1977 I was born. In August of 1977 I was born. On 16[h] August, 1977 I was born in West Bengal.
At	Specific point of time	He wakes up 3 o'clock everyday.
By	Before the time	By noon I'll finish this task.
During	To mean season or period of time	During morning walk I met her hundred times. During school days she was my best friend.
For	For a period of time, in all tense.	He was sleeping for ten hours. I am working here for last twenty years.
From	Starting from particular time	From seventeen she was in love with me, and we didn't get married. Marriage is not last word in love.
Since	Mainly to use in perfect tense	He has been working in this project since last year. Since Monday she is in ill.
Within	Before the specific time	We'll reach within two hours. Within five days you must complete this work.

3. Preposition that indicates '**Movement**' or '**Motion**', i.e., form the adverb of Movement; as,

3. Preposition that indicates 'Movement' or 'Motion'

Prepositions	Examples
Through	We are walking through the jungle and not know the end.
Across	He ran across the road & slightly saved from the accident.
Along	Peter walked along the beach road and enjoyed scenic beauty.
Past	The car went past me.
Above	The kite is flying **above** the tress.
Over	The dog jumps over the table.
To , Into	The dog fell into the ditch. The boy goes to school.
About	The sailor went about the world.
Towards	We travelled towards Nasik after this.
Up	The thief climbed up the ladder & stole into the room.
Down	I came (got) down from the running bus.

4. Prepositions of **Direction**:

Some prepositions show where something is going. They are adverb in nature or form Adverb of Direction: as,

- The boys chased ***after*** each other.
- The football rolled ***down*** the hill.
- A man was walking his dog ***along*** the riverbank.
- The freeway goes ***right*** through the city.
- We were travelling ***towards*** Miami.

❏ Prepositions that show 'Direction'

Prepositions	Prepositions that show 'Direction', almost similar to 'motion', but have difference. Study them carefully.
To	Turn to him and say whatever you have concern or grievance.
Towards	Nicky turned towards north & started hi journey again.
From	Don't let your attention to divert from this point.
Into	He entered the room. He came into the room.
At	He looked at me & said nothing.
In	He went in the east of the country. (In east part) He went to the east. (Merely direction, towards east) He went at the east of the country. (At last point)

5. Preposition that indicates '**Agent/Instrument /Manner**' (including measure, standard, rate, value, etc.)

	Examples
By	Send the parcel by post. It was destroyed by fire. I was stunned by the sudden blow.
With	Cut the cake with a knife.
Through	I heard of this news through one of my friends.
At	Sell good s at auction. (It means agency more than a place) The bank charges interest at eight percent. Stories like these must be taken at what they are worth.

Prepositions that show Manner:

By	The patient was dying by inches since last August. Cloth is sold by the yard. I am taller than you by two inches. It was one by the tower clock.

| With | The soldiers fought with courage.
They won the battle with ease.
They worked on it with earnestness. |

6. Prepositions that show **Cause, Reason** or **Purpose'**

	Examples
For	o Everyone should labour for the good of humanity. o It is a place for a picnic. He took medicine for cold.
From	o She has been suffering from gout. o No one died from fatigue. However, it is a popular illusion.
Of	o Shyam, my friend died of fever.
With	o She shivers with fever.
Pending	o She was held in custody **pending** trial.
In	o My father died in accident. o Many died in cholera in the last famine.
Through	o The soldier retreated through fear of an ambush. (Due to the cause of his fear; don't confuse it with manner; and thus:) o You have lost your purse through negligence. (For the cause of). o He concealed his talent through shame. Lockdown gave him a chance.

7. **Contrast & Concession**
- o After (in spite of, notwithstanding) every effort, one may fail.
- o For (in place of) one enemy he has a hundred friends.
- o For (in spite of) all his wealth he is not content.
- o With (in spite of) all his faults I admire him.

8. **Inference, motive, source, or origin**
- o *From* what I know of him, I hesitate to trust him.
- o The knights were brave *from* gallantry of spirit.
- o He did it *from* gratitude.
- o Light emanates *from* the sun.
- o From labor health, *from* health contentment springs.

- This is a quotation *from* Milton.
- His skill comes *from* practice.
- He comes *of* a good family.
- It was good *of* you to help me.
- He has come *from* a royal family.

- **Exercise-1:** <u>Identify the Functions of Prepositions in the following</u> <u>sentences:</u>
  - There is a cow **in the field.** (It denotes 'place of adverb', denoting the position of the cow.)
  - He is fond **of tea**. (It has formed the complement of adjective, 'fond'.)
  - The cat jumped **off the chair**. (Denotes adverb of movement, adds meaning to the word, 'jumped')
  - *We* shall have a Transparency Integrity seminar **in** August (time)
  - The boys are sitting **under** a tree
  - Girl is sitting **on** the table
  - The visitors are walking **round** the school(direction)
  - Our principal will travel **by** train(method)
  - Rubi was <u>behind</u> the tree.
  - I was standing in front of the tree.
  - Tima is walking **towards** the borehole.
  - Grace threw the ball **into** the bucket.
  - The boy was seen going **through** the fence.
  - She was standing in front of the tree.
  - Tima is walking **towards** the borehole.
  - Grace threw the ball **into** the bucket.
  - The boy was seen going **through** the fence.

Some prepositions need special attention:

1) **Usage of 'at':** *(for exact location, near at small place, at exact time, & many others); as,*
   - We started at eight o'clock. At any time, I am ready to go.
   - He woke up at dawn. At day time we do our work. (**Also:** in the dawn, in the day time, during day time)
   - Why to sing so loudly at bed-time? Eat this one at a time.
   - They are at work. The boys are at play now.
   - He is now at home/at school/at his office.
   - He was at the door, when he heard her cry for help.
   - We were at dinner, then my aunt visited us.

- Suddenly I fell at sea. Feel at home, we are like your own.
- He ran at full speed, and yet was beat by others on the track. He was standing at a distance when I saw him. He is at the meeting.
- He studied at this university. Everyone is asked to present at the meeting at a short notice. The professor shouted at the boys.
- I did not expect such treatment at your hands (from you)
- Look at me. He is very good at cricket. He is seen at all places.
- We will hear at the latest by Saturday. At any moment he may come.
- This can be found at all places. At age of sixty he married again.

2) **Usage of 'by':** *(when we talk about **'means of transport'** to mean **'an agent of an action that may be person or thing'** & to mean **'manner of doing an action'** we use 'by' before the noun & preceding a verb.)*
- We travelled by train. (Not: by the or by a train); and thus, travelling by boat, ship, plane or by air & by car, etc.;
- By day time I don't go sleep, but only at night.
- What is your routine in the day and in the night?
- The machine was driven by steam (by electricity or by petrol).
- It was destroyed by fire, not by earthquake.
- Send him the message by telegram.
- I know him by sight everyday morning while I myself go out.
- Students like teaching by suitable examples by teacher.
- By next Sunday we will reach there.
- She is indomitable by word of mouth.
- He studied his lessen by heart. Send this letter by post for me.
- By chance they met and fell in love to each other.
- Sell things by kilogram or meter, keep the calculation in hand always.
- He died by poison (by accident). She is older by five months.
- Eggs are sold by dozen. Sit by me. I did this work all by myself.
- It is 10-30 by my watch. Pay the amount by NEFT please.
- Everyone was struck by sudden lighting.
- This room is ten by fifteen feet. We live by the river.

3) **Usage of in:** *(before a **big town, region, country, state, district**, etc.; and as time of preposition, it is used before **year, month**, etc.); as,*
- I was born in 1986. In last holiday we went there.
- They lived in Canada. It was written in ink.
- It was happened in last February.

- The town is in ruins now. In every afternoon they walk along.
- His party is n power now. I sat in arm chair.
- You were in haste to buy the scooter.
- Be careful to fall in danger. She was in pain, I saved her.
- I was in difficulty; he helped me to out from there.
- The people are in arms against the king.
- She threw dust in my eyes, none realized this.
- Wait, I am coming back in five minutes.
- He came in time. Fill in the forms. Fill in the blanks.

4) **Usage of 'on':** (on particular date, occasion, place or upper surface, on banks of river, hanging on something, and to mean 'specific transport'). **Note:** We already said for transport we use **'by'**; but, when we mean walking or cycling or any 'specific transport', we use **'on'** or **'in'** in place of 'by'. Carefully study the examples:

- I travelled two kilometers on horseback & three kilometers on a bicycle on rent.
- We reached the peak climbing on rough hills.
- He goes to office on foot. I went there on bicycle.
- Suresh went there on my bike.
- We travelled in Mr. Joshi's car. They came in a taxi.
- I'll go on the 7.30 bus in the morning.
- On Wednesday my child was born.
- On 16th August, he joined his job.
- He was lying on bed. Write an essay on the topic/subject.
- The house was on fire. On oath I say, I didn't take yours.
- He is on the way to office. He was on time always.
- He is sitting on the sofa. The train is running on time.
  - My uncle came on holiday. It was on left.
  - Kolkata is on the Hooghly.
  - He lectured on a common topic
  - We live on rice. We live on our small income.
- He is playing on a musical instrument.
- He is on that committee. (Not: in)
- Our house is on the main road. It is on the Bhanumati Road.
- There is hanging a picture on the wall.
- I had a ring on my finger. Now I am listening news on TV.
- Balurghat is on the north of India. It was done on request/on demand.
- No animal on land, on sea or in air is as large as a blue whale.
- The car is on hire. He was on trial. I met him on the road.

o   We walk on foot. It is nice to look a fruit on the tree. I am on duty.

5) **Usage of 'Of'** (*to show related something, parts of or possession*):
   o   Our modules are full ***of*** real-life examples.
   o   I ate a plate ***of*** rice and a quarter ***of*** milk.
   o   Would you like a glass ***of*** lemon juice?
   o   I need three pieces ***of*** paper.
   o   Most ***of*** the children in my class like Education.
   o   There are several ways ***of*** cooking Upma.
   o   The Museum ***of*** Balurghat was not visited by me ever.
   o   My father was a man ***of*** means, and he gathered money not more than penny.
   o   Do not lose sight ***of*** the fact.
   o   I had cured ***of*** illness finally.

6) **Usage of 'for':** (*mainly to show cause, reason, allotted for or availability*); *as,*
   o   I made this bookmark ***for*** Mom.
   o   She was crying out ***for*** fear.
   o   Is there room ***for*** me on this seat? (To mean 'availability')
   o   This house is ***for*** sale.
   o   I'd like a new computer ***for*** Christmas. (To mean 'on the occasion of' rather than cause')
   o   It is time ***for*** going out.
   o   We're going down town ***for*** a meeting.
   o   We bought a white Hyundai car ***for*** Rupees seven lakhs.
   o   I made this gift ***for*** my mother.
   o   You are unfit ***for*** the post.
   o   Is there place ***for*** me on this seat?
   o   I am getting ready ***for*** school.
   o   I'd like a new Laptop ***for*** Next year.
   o   Why has he got the draft ***for*** Rupees ten lakhs?

7) **Usage of 'Than':** *'than' is often regarded as preposition when it is used before a noun or pronoun and show relation with other; used in comparative degree and also to mean* **'except'**; *as,*
   o   My backpack is bigger ***than*** John's.
   o   Dad is taller ***than*** all of us.
   o   This painting is more beautiful ***than*** that one.
   o   The neighborhood streets are less busy ***than*** downtown streets.

- o   A stone is heavy, and sand is weighty; but a fool's wrath is heavier than them both.
- o   The shop keeper refused to accept less than ten rupees for the soap.
- o   No one other than a graduate need/can apply. (except)
- o   She did nothing else than cry. (than = except)

8) **Usage of 'with':** *(to show <u>essential parts of</u> or the <u>instrument for an action with</u>, <u>mix something with</u> other, <u>accompany with</u>, etc.); as,*
- o   He pounds nails ***with*** a hammer.
- o   Mix the flour ***with*** water.
- o   She painted the picture ***with*** her new paints.
- o   Would you like to come ***with*** us to the cinema? (Give company)
- o   I can do difficult problems ***with*** help from Mom.
- o   Who is the man ***with*** the beard?
- o   The boy ***with*** red hair I met last Sunday at temple.

9) **Usage of 'in', 'at'** (when they denote place, '**in**' is used for larger or bigger region, '**at**' for small region):
- o   Mr. Peter lives in West Bengal.
- o   I live at Balurghat.

Note: We use 'in' with the names of streets and 'at' when we give the house-number:
- o   He lives in Park Street.
- o   He lives at 26B, Gayeshwar Sarani Lane.

10) **In, at, to, into** ('in' or 'at' are used to denote rest position; while '**to**', '**into**' for motion):
- o   The snake is in the hole. He is in his room.
- o   Where do you live at? He is at the door.
- o   The snake scrawls into the hole. He goes into the room.
- o   The boy goes to school.

11) **On, upon** ('on' is used to mean something is at rest on the upper surface; while '**upon**' for both upon surface at rest or in motion):
- o   The baby sits on/upon the mother's lap. (Rest position but on upper surface)
- o   The cat jumped upon the table. ('motion' position)

12) **With, by:** 'with' is used for the thing (instrument) with which something is done; while 'by' for the person or animal (agent) who

does the thing; as,
- o He killed the snake with an iron rod.
- o The snake was killed by the peasant.

13) **In, on, within, after:**
   a) 'In time' denotes 'not late, early enough';
   b) 'On time' denotes 'at the appointed time'; meaning at the close of;
   c) 'within' refers to 'before the close of time'&
   d) 'after' refers to 'over the period of time'; as,
   - o She will return in twenty-four hours. (Early enough before twenty-four hours) /she will return in time.
   - o She will return on a day. (At the appointed time; not late & not early)
   - o She will return within a week's time. (Before the close of week)
   - o She will return after a week's time. (After the week)

14) **Between, among:** between is used in case of two persons; while among is used in case of more than two persons; as,
   - o The two thieves shared the booty between themselves.
   - o The four thieves sat in a cave to distribute the booty among them.

15) **Before, for:** 'before' to mean 'earlier of a point of time'; while 'for' is used to mean \'for a space of time'; as,
   - o He will be here before six o'clock.
   - o He will not be here for an hour.

16) **Since, from:** both are used to denote 'a point of time', while 'since' is used in the perfect tenses, 'from' is used in any tense (though not so rigid in present days); as,
   - o She will begin to learn Sanskrit from to-morrow.
   - o She has been suffering from fever since Monday last.

17) **By, since, before:** 'by' to mean 'near about the point of time', 'since' from point of time' & 'before' is used to denote earlier than the point of time; as,
   - o She wants to come back *by* seven o'clock in the evening.
   - o She has been here *since* four o'clock in afternoon.
   - o She could not come back *before* ten o'clock at night.

18) **'But',** as a preposition is used to mean '**except**'; **'instead of'** is

used to mean '*in place of*' something; as,

- I like all kinds of food **_except_** Upma. (But Upma)
- Everyone likes chocolate **_except_** Tom. (But Tom)
- We go to school every day **_except_** Saturday and Sunday. (Leaving Saturday & Sunday)
- You should eat fruit **_instead of_** candy. (In place of)
- Dad is coming to the theater with us **_instead of_** Mom.
- We could watch TV **_instead of_** reading our books.
- All the girls in class-X passed **_but_** (except) one.

19) **Beside, besides:** 'beside' denotes '*at or by the side of*' or 'outside of'; 'besides' denotes '**in addition to**'; as,

- She came & sat beside me. (By my side)
- Beside the village, there flows a small stream. (By the side of/ outside of)
- Your answer is beside the question. (Outside of/irrelevant to)
- Besides his friends, his neighbors also came to his help. (In addition to)

20) The preposition **'a'** as the shortened form of **'on'** & **'o'** as the shortened form of **'of'** is used like the following:

- I wake up 3 **_o_**'clock (3 of the clock).
- The tutor comes here twice **_a_** week (twice on a week).

21) The word **'like'** is used as a preposition to mean **'as**. Study the examples:

- Kathleen looks **_like_** her dad.
- Andrew smiles **_like_** his mother.
- Peter sings **_like_** a professional singer and his son Om **_as_** a pop.
- Are these shoes the same **_as_** those on the rack?
- Sue is nearly as tall **_as_** the teacher.
- He is stupid **_as_** his brother.

Exercise-2: **_Mark out the function of prepositions:_**

- He works **in an office**. (As adverbials)
- The boy **with a blue shirt** came here. (As post modifier)
- I congratulate you **on your success**. (As verb complement)
- I am good **at counting**. (As adjective complement)

The Place of Prepositions

Like adverb, preposition has no such definite place to be used; rather, they can be used at anywhere. However, <u>generally it is used before a noun or a pronoun or a noun equivalent word</u> and <u>shows</u> a *relation of that noun* or pronoun *with any other noun, verb or adjective*. <u>Sometimes, with a noun it forms adverbial phrase or adverb</u>, and <u>using with a verb it forms phrasal verbs</u>; and thus, it is sometimes used at the end of a sentence. Study the following for further understanding.

1) A Prepositions is ***used before its object*** that may be a Noun, Pronoun, Adverbial Phrase or a Clause; as,
   → My younger brother is reading ***in*** <u>class vii</u>.
   → The pet cat drinks the milk ***from*** <u>milk pot</u>.
   → I placed the cheque book ***before*** <u>him</u>.
   → She must read ***by*** then. (It is an adverbial phrase

   Note: Of first three sentences the underlined are the Prepositional Objects. when of the last one '***by then***' is an adverbial phrase, denoting time.

2) When an object to a preposition preceding a Relative Pronoun *(who, whom, that, etc. and they may be understood too)*, the preposition is ***used at the end of the sentence***; as,
   → Here is <u>the book</u> that he asked ***for***.
   → This is the <u>stolen watch</u> that the police were searching ***for***.
   → That is <u>the man</u> whom I spoke ***of***.
   → That is <u>the boy</u> (whom) I was speaking ***of***.
   → Here is <u>the watch</u> that you asked ***for***.

3) When an object to a preposition is a part of Interrogative Pronoun (what for, where from, etc.), the preposition is ***placed at the end of the sentence***; as,
   → <u>What</u> are you searching ***for***?
   → <u>Where</u> the traveler does come ***from***?
   → <u>Who</u> (whom) do you want to speak ***to***?
   → <u>What</u> are you looking ***at***?
   → <u>What</u> are you thinking ***of***?
   → <u>Which of these chairs</u> did you sit ***on***?

4) Sometimes to give emphasis on an object (or as part of an emotion to express), the preposition is ***placed at the end*** *& the object is placed before it or is placed first in the sentence*; as,
- → The young novelist is known all the <u>world</u> **over**. (known all over the world).
- → <u>This</u> I was talking **about**.
- → <u>This</u> I insist **on**.
- → He is known the entire <u>world</u> **over**. (known over the entire world)

5) In a passive structure, when the verb is emphasized, the preposition may be used ***at the end of the sentence;*** as,
- → The bed has not been **slept in**. (No one has slept in the bed.)
- → I hate being **laughed at**. (They are laughing at me, I hate it.)
- → When an object of the verb is emphasized, the object set or comes before the main verb which becomes an infinitive verb& with the infinitive the preposition is ***placed at the end***; as,
- → It is a <u>nice place</u> **to live in**. (We live in this nice place.)
- → He needs <u>other boys</u> **to play with**. (He plays with other boys.)

⊿ *Summary of, When Prepositions used at the end:*

1) When relative Pronoun is used:
- → That is **what** I am afraid **of**.
- → This is the house **that** she lived **in**.
- → Tom was the person **whom** he talked **to**.

2) When interrogative Pronoun is used:
- → **What** are you looking **at**?
- → **Where** did you buy it **from**?
- → **What** did you say that **for**?

3) In passive structures:
- → The bed has not been **slept in**.
- → I hate being **laughed at**.
- → It was not that to be **aimed at**.
- → I am not that beauty to get being **stared at**.

4) Often in infinitive structures:
- → It is a nice place **to live in**.
- → He needs other boys **to play with**.
- → It was not such a matter **to deal in**.

→ He was not that man **to deal with**.

5) When prepositional objects are emphasized:
→ <u>This</u> you were looking *for*.
→ <u>This</u> I was talking ***about***.
→ He is known all the <u>world</u> ***over***.

Prepositional Object or Complement

❑ A preposition does not stand alone but needs a word or words to move on or to complete its sense, which is usually a **noun** or a **pronoun,** a **phrase of adverbial accusative** or a **clausal structure** [like '–<u>ing</u>' <u>clause</u> or 'wh-' clause, etc.]; as,
→ I listened **to** <u>you</u> attentively.
(Here, preposition **'to'** shows relation between **'you'**, a pronoun with a verb, **'listened'**. **'You'** is <u>the object of the preposition</u> **'to'**, getting the answer with the question **'to whom/whom?'** In other case, the answers to the questions— **'what for'**, **'to what'**, **'where'**, **'at what time'** are also other examples of prepositional objects. Some prepositional objects are also termed as Indirect objects, though not all. Study the chapter of object or Transitive and Intransitive verbs). Read here the rest of Prepositional Objects.
→ He gave the pen ***to*** <u>Rakesh</u>. (Whom did he give the pen = to Rakesh. The underlined is the prepositional object.)
→ We moved on ***towards*** <u>the final peak</u> ***of*** <u>mountain</u>. (Towards what?)
→ I saw a girl ***in*** <u>the garden</u>. (Where?)
→ ***Until*** <u>now</u> nothing happens. (until when?)
→ ***By*** <u>then</u> I was merely twenty-one; when I was seduced ***by*** <u>a woman</u>.
  ❑ In the above, the underlined are the complements of their preceding prepositions. **'Then'** is an adverb, **'by then'** an adverbial phrase; when 'a woman' is a noun phrase; here an agent of an action.

○ Know the **objects** or **complements** of Prepositions in the following sentences:
1) Consider **Noun or Pronouns as Objects** to a Preposition: The preposition may take single or double objects; as,
  ○ I place my book ***on*** <u>the table</u>. Don't insist ***on*** <u>me</u>.

- o I saw a girl **in** the garden watering the plants.
- o The dry leaves fall **from** the trees.
- o The calf runs **over** fields & gardens.
- o The road **run** over hill & plain.

2) While, **Adverbs** are suggested to consider as **Complements to the preposition** when a preposition governs on them; as,
- o She must be tired **by** then. (By that time)
- o She must have reached there **by** now. (By this time)
- o Come away **from** there. (From that place).
- o How far is it **from** here (this place)?
- o **Until** now it as not ceased raining.
- o Strange things happen **between** now & then.
- o The brook says, 'I go on **for**ever.' It cannot last **for**ever.

3) **Phrase as Objects or Complements:** 'to whom', 'to what' are questions to have Prepositional Objects, when other 'wh' words helps to find out complements to the Prepositions.
- ✠ A Noun Phrase may be an object or a complement to the preposition, but an Adverbial phrase is mostly a complement to a Preposition; as,
  - o I bought the article **for** under half its value.
  - o The old bottle is sold **at** over one rupee each.
  - o Mr. Basu was not promoted to the post of Accounts Officer **till** within a few months of his retirement.
  - o I did not see her **till** a few months ago.
  - o The smoke was coming **from** across the field.
  - o I was thinking **about** how to circumvent him.

4) **Clause as Objects:** A Noun Clause like a Noun or Pronoun may be the object or a complement to a Preposition, like a phrase does; as,
- o Pay careful attention **to** what I am doing. (As object to preposition)
- o There is no sense **in** what he says. (As object to preposition)

Omission of Object to a Preposition

The Object to a Preposition is omitted when the object is a-
  - **a)** Relative Pronoun:
    - ▪ The boy (whom) we were looking for has come.
    - ▪ These are the good rules (which) to live by.

b) Demonstrative Pronoun:
- Here is a chair to sit on (it/the chair).
- There was a river to drink from. (That river)

c) Where sense is evident without object, one preposition is also omitted with the object:
- Get up (from bed). Get out (from here.)
- Sit down (on the chair/ on the bench/ on bed), etc.

When preposition itself is omitted

- The Prepositions— *for, from, in, on* —are often <u>omitted from the adverbial phrase of</u> **Place**, **Distance** & **Time**; as,
  - We did it *(in)* last week.
  - I can't walk *(for)* a yard.
  - Wait *(for)* a minute.
- ❏ If after such verbs as **come, go, arrive, get, send, take, bring**— the word **home** is used as an adverb, we do not need any preposition.

- ❏ Study the table of 'use of prepositions' & 'without use of prepositions':

Without prepositions	With prepositions
1) He **comes home** at 5 o'clock.	1) He **comes to me** at 5 o'clock.
2) The boy **goes home** at 4 p.m.	2) He **goes to market** at 4 o'clock.
3) We hope to **arrive home** at night.	3) The boss **arrives at office** in time.
4) They **got home** a kitten.	4) I **got to fly a kite**.
5) **Send him his home**.	5) **Send this parcel to Mr. Biswas**.
6) Kindly **take me your home**.	6) Kindly **take this application to** consider.
7) **Bring home** a CD player and enjoy music.	7) **Bring a CD player to enjoy** music.

- ❏ After verbs like **discuss, enter,** and time expressing words like **next, last, this, one, every, each, some, any**—we do not use any prepositions; as,
  - We **discussed** the matter.
  - The dacoits **entered** the house.

- o **Next Tuesday** you will go there.
- o **Last month** we visited Taj Mahal.
- o **This morning** I went the temple.
- o Only **one hour** I read.
- o **Every Sunday** we go to temple.
- o **Each moment** is valuable.
- o **Some time** I enjoyed the music.
- o **Any evening** you visit there.

❑ **Study again another table of 'use of prepositions' & 'without use of prepositions':**

Without prepositions	With prepositions
1) We **discussed** the matter.	1) We **talked about** the matter.
2) The dacoits **entered** the house.	2) The dacoits **went into** the house.
3) **Next Tuesday** you will go there.	3) You will go there **on Tuesday** after.
4) **Last month** we visited Taj Mahal.	4) We visited Taj Mahal **the month before**.
5) **This morning** I went the temple.	5) I went the temple **in the morning**.
6) Only **one hour** I read.	6) I have read only **for an hour**.
7) **Every Sunday** we go to temple.	7) We go to temple **on Sundays**.
8) **Each moment** is valuable.	8) I am not sorry **for the moment**.
9) **Some time** I enjoyed music.	9) I enjoyed it **for some reason**.
10) **Any evening** you may visit there.	10) You may visit there **in the evening**.

Same words may be used as both **Adverbs** & **Prepositions.** We said already a part of speech may be used as other part of speech in a sentence and that (their functions or use) defines their name or identity. Study the followings:

When they are adverbs	When they are prepositions
1) Go & run *about*.	1) Don't loiter *about* in the corridor.
2) Let us move *on*.	
3) Come *down*.	2) The book lies *on* the table.
4) The bullock cart moves *on*.	3) We went *down* the slopes of the hills.
5) Three men passed *by*.	4) The cat sat *on* the wall outside.
6) The rain falls *without.*	5) She sat *by* the cottage door.

7) They left the weak man **behind**.	6) Man cannot live **without** bread.
8) I could not come **before**.	7) The black cat hid **behind** the door.
9) Has she come **in**?	8) I came the day **before** yesterday.
10) The wheel came **off**.	9) Is he **in** his room?
11) His father arrived soon **after**.	10) The driver jumped **off** the car?
12) Take this parcel **over** to the post office.	11) **After** a month he returned.
13) I have not seen him **since**.	12) He rules **over** a vast empire.
	13) I have not slept **since** yesterday.
Note: adverbs when it merely modifies.	*Note:* Prepositions when it governs nouns or pronouns besides modify or form adv. Ph.

○ **Important Notes-The characteristics what we might note:**
(1) Prepositions are generally used before Nouns or Pronouns, but remember, prepositions are also used with adjective or participles & verbs, like in the following sentences, no- 2 & 3. They are used with 'fond', an adjective; and 'jumped', a verb.

    1. There is a cow **in** the field.
    2. He is fond **of** tea.
    3. The cat jumped **off** the chair.

- *In sentence 1*, the word '*in*' is placed before '*the field*' (mainly 'field'; 'the' is an article to define 'field') & *shows relation between two words,* **'cow' & 'field' (both are Nouns)**.

- *In sentence 2*, the word '*of*' is placed before '*tea*' & *shows relation between two words,* **'fond' & 'tea' (Adj.& Noun)**.

- *In sentence 3*, the word '*off*' is placed before '*the chair*' (mainly 'chair') & thus *shows relation between the two words,* **'jumped' & 'chair' (Verb & Noun)**.

- **Note:** Thus, Prepositions generally used before Nouns and they show relation with other words that may be another Noun, or an Adjective or a Verb, like the above.
- Here, the words— *in, of, off* —are the examples of Prepositions.

(2) The Nouns or Pronouns which are used after the prepositions, are called its Object, (the Object of the Preposition); and they are always in the Accusative Case.

> **Note:** Where Normal Objects (objects of Transitive Verbs, Direct & Indirect), Object of Gerund, Infinitive, Participle— can be used in the Nominative Case when they are used as subjects; however, Prepositional Objects are always in the Accusative Case. Study the examples carefully.

(3) Prepositions along with other words, are often used to form different phrases as **Noun phrase, adjective phrase, phrasal Verbs, adverbial phrase** & **phrase of preposition**, etc.

(4) Certain Nouns, Adjectives, Participles & Verbs are always followed by particular Prepositions.

> ➢ Now, we will go through the last feature in details.

Conjugation of Preposition with Other Parts of Speech

Certain Nouns, Adjectives, Participles & Verbs are always followed by particular Prepositions.

A. Certain **Nouns** which are followed by '*for*' Preposition:

1) She had **affection for** none. Don't' cherish **anxiety for** others.
2) In young hood I had **ambition for** becoming a writer, alas! I could become none.
3) I seek **apology for** my fault; yet, she hardly forgives me. She says, it is too frequent.
4) I had no **appetite for** your love, yet you pushed me thousand times.
5) The public have insatiable **appetite for** scandal.
6) You have no **aptitude for** this job. I am sorry.
7) Why do you **blame for**? The tank has no **capacity for** thousand liters.
8) We urgently **need** candidates **for** the recruitment. Make fast the process, C.M.'s order.

9) She was such a noble and kind woman had **compassion** even *for* a dead rat.

10) They sought **compensation for** their loss, we had hardly anything.

11) Your **contempt for** women will make you soon hateful among netizens.

12) There is still no **cure for** the common cold.

13) Little Jack proved quite a **match for** the giant.

❑ And thus, *craving, desire, esteem, fitness, fondness, guarantee, leisure, liking, match, motive, need, opportunity, partiality, passion, pity, prediction, pretext, relish, remorse, reputation, surety*— all the nouns take *'for'* preposition after them.

B.   Certain **Nouns** which are mainly followed by '**with**':

14) I have no **acquaintance with** this man, believe me.

15) Regarding this, the country has an **alliance with** Japan.

16) I hate **bargain with** beggars. Have any **comparison with** the two?

17) If had this **conformity with** the declaration by the Government, but alas, we are left for none.

18) What have you **enmity with** him? Resolve that soon.

19) She had **intercourse with** her boyfriend, she proudly admitted.

20) Why is this **intimacy with** him and all these behind your husband?

21) I have no **relation with** her any longer. We are departed since last year.

22) He made **complaint with** the Principal ma'am against her room-mates in drunk.

C.   Certain **Nouns** which are mainly followed by '**of**

23) The celebrated grammarian Patanjali was a **contemporary of** Pushyamitra Sunga.

24) I give **assurance of** surety, no problem. He was **in charge of** the police station.

25) **Distrust of** humanity is a wrong idea for your own existence.

26) They have **doubt of** our projects and schemes. What's next?

27) Sorry sir, I have no **experience of** teachings, see other.

28) **Failure of** goal jumps to give lecture!

29) Keep **observance of** her progress and inform us in time.

30) Have you any **proof of** my guilt? If no, think next time thousand before jump.

31) We were eagerly **waiting for** our result, and the **result of** MBA was declared postponed.
32) They may have **want of** money, but they are not scoundrel.
33) The President **called for** an immediate **cessation of** hostilities among the communities in West India.

D. Certain **Nouns** which are mainly followed by '**to**'

34) We have no **access to** the basement.
35) The then people celebrated Charles I's **accession to** the throne.
36) He affirmed his **allegiance to** the President.
37) It is **alternative to** that medicine.
38) Have you **antidote to** that disease?
39) The citizens grow **antipathy to** (also: towards) the new Act of Government.
40) We shouldn't **approach to** this proposal. It seems **risky for** us.
41) The director has given her **assent to** the proposal.
42) Mother has always special **attachment to** her elder child.
43) Please, give your **attention to** me.
44) You'll get 5% **concession to** the total price of this item.
45) It was **disgrace to** his dignity and he showed his power over us.
46) Pitila has **dislike to** tea. We had no **enmity to** anyone.
47) Give **encouragement to** your child to submit projects on time.
48) It was **exception to** his nature, or he is very fine, cool & temperate.

❑ And thus, *incentive, indifference, invitation, key, leniency, likeness, limit, menace, obedience, objection, obstruction, opposition, postscript, preface, reference, repugnance, resemblance, sequel, submission, succession, supplement, temptation, traitor*— all the nouns take '*to*' preposition after them.

E. Certain **Nouns** which are mainly followed by '***from***'

49) Buddhism teaches that **freedom from** desires will lead to **escape from** suffering.
50) You need total **abstinence from** drink, if you want to live.
51) He sighed long after **deliverance from** sure death.
52) His **digression from** main point is too disgusting to run the conversation.
53) She was given **exemption from** the final examination.
54) The President is given **exemption from** paying tax to the Govt.
55) Her **inference from** ignorancc to knowledge is sufficient reason to give her appointment.

56) I need some ***respite from*** this tiresome job.
57) He traces his line of ***descent from*** the Maurya kings.
- ❏ **Note:** *when it means 'ancestry or family origin' it takes 'from'; but when it means 'a slope going downward', it takes 'to'; when it means 'coming or going down' it takes 'into' after it; as,*
58) There is a gradual ***descent to*** the sea.
59) The country's swift ***descent into*** anarchy was bad luck for the countrymen.

Conjugation of Preposition with Participle or Adjectives:

A. Certain ***Adjectives or Participles*** which are followed by Preposition ***'to'***

60) These computers are cheap enough to be ***accessible to*** most people.
61) It was ***adequate to*** meet our needs, but we are undone even with it.
62) The house was ***adjacent to*** the post office.
63) The true gentleman is courteous and ***affable to*** his neighbors.
64) Be ***affectionate to*** your younger brother.
65) Neither was ***akin to*** us. Everything was ***alien to*** our knowledge.
66) Still, he is ***alive to*** his citizens. Why are you ***callous to*** everything?
67) It is ***common to*** every mortal man.
68) He I ***contrary to*** his younger brother.
69) Few things are ***impossible to*** diligence and skill.
70) His duties were of a kind ***ill-suited to*** his ardent and daring character.
71) Newly acquired freedom is sometimes ***liable to*** abuse.
72) He (Dr. Johnson) was somewhat ***susceptible to*** flattery.

B. Certain ***Adjectives or Participles*** which are followed by Preposition ***'to'***

73) It was formerly supposed that malaria was ***due to poisonous*** exhalations.
74) The students are ***obedient to*** their teachers. It was relevant to the treaty.
75) People who are ***averse to*** hard work, generally do not <u>succeed **in**</u> life. (1st one adjective, 2nd one verb),
76) She is determined to marry that rascal, what can we do her poor parents?

❑ **And thus,** abhorrent, acceptable, agreeable, amendable, analogous, applicable, appropriate, beneficial, comparable, condemned, conducive, conformable, comfortable, consistent, congenial, consecrated, contrary, creditable, deaf, derogatory, detrimental, devoted, disastrous, entitles, equal, essential, exposed, faithful, fatal, foreign, hostile, impertinent, incidental, inclined, indebted, indifferent, indispensable, indulgent, inimical, insensible, injured, irrelevant, favorable, hurtful, immaterial, hurtful, impervious, indigenous, limited, lost, loyal, material, natural, necessary, obliged, offensive, opposite, painful, partial, peculiar, pertinent, pledged, preferable, prejudicial, prior, profitable, prone, reduced, related, relevant, repugnant, responsible, restricted, sacred, sensitive, serviceable, subject, suitable, suited, supplementary, tantamount, true, etc., — all the adjectives or participles take *'to'* preposition after them.

    C. Certain ***Adjectives or Participles*** which are followed by Preposition *'in'*

77) He is ***absorbed in*** her thoughts. He is in love.
78) You were ***accurate in*** calculation. They stuck ***surprised by*** your talent.
79) I am from ***backward in*** class as per your class division.
80) Peter was ***correct in*** his assumption.
81) The car was ***defective in*** engine.
82) He was ***deficient in*** management.
83) We are not ***experienced in*** this field.
84) He is ***honest in*** his words; we should believe him.
85) I am not ***interested in*** cycling, but it is ***good for*** health.
86) How did you come ***involved in*** this thing?
87) Be ***temperate in*** thoughts and action, success is at your feet.

❑ **And thus,** abstemious, accomplished, assiduous, bigoted, diligent, enveloped, fertile, foiled, implicated, lax, proficient, remiss, versed, etc.— all the adjectives take *'in'* preposition after them.

    D. Certain ***Adjectives or Participles*** which are followed by Preposition *'with'*

88) I am ***acquainted with*** the President, let me go in, sir, or inform him about my presence. Tell him Peter has come.
89) He was ***afflicted with*** sorrow and told us, 'No'.
90) Let's get ***busy with*** clearing up.

91) I'll be ***busy to*** come to the meeting. She was ***busy to*** listen news on TV.

92) The Dr. is ***busy at*** the moment. Gomez was ***busy at*** her work.

93) He was contemporary with the dramatist Congreve.

94) The guests were ***contented with*** the service.

95) Emily was ***delighted with*** her success or achievement.

96) The text color is ***contrasted with*** its background color.

97) Jayden was ***gifted with*** his remarkable I.Q.

98) It was ***infected with*** poison. We are ***inspired with*** his advice.

99) He was very ***popular with*** his fans and followers.

100) Was she ***satiated with*** her desires? I am ***satisfied with*** my achievement.

101) India is a noble, gorgeous land, ***teeming with*** natural wealth.

❑ And thus, beset, compatible, compliant, conversant, convulsed, deluged, disgusted, drenched, endowed, fatigued, fired, infatuated, infested, intimate, invested, overcome, replete, touched, etc. — all the adjectives take *'with'* preposition after them.

    E. Certain ***Adjectives or Participles*** which are followed by Preposition *'of'*

102) Annikesh was ***accused of*** illegal love ***affair with*** his ex-student, Priya.

103) However, he was ***acquitted of*** all charges, and sent to an asylum considering his mental health.

104) Of course, I am not ***afraid of*** you or anybody you call.

105) I was little ***apprehensive of*** the effects.

106) Being ***apprised of*** our approach, the whole neighborhood came out to meet their minister.

107) We were ***assured of*** the best service. Do you ***aware of*** this?

108) They were not ***cautious of*** the coming danger. He should not be ***deprived of*** his right. It was ***destitute of*** his fate that he did not pass.

109) Naples was then destitute ***of*** what are now, perhaps, its chief attractions.

110) Why do you envious of them?

111) Jawaharlal Nehru was ***fond of*** children.

112) He is a man of deep learning, but totally ***ignorant of*** life and manners.

113) Ashoka, although ***tolerant of*** competing creeds, was personally an ardent Buddhist.

❑ And thus, bereft, bought, certain, characteristic, composed, confident, conscious, convicted, convinced, covetous, defrauded, desirous, devoid, diffident, distrustful, dull, easy, fearful, greedy, guilty, heedless, informed, innocent, irrespective, lame, lavish, negligent, productive, proud, regardless, sanguine, sensible, sick, slow, subversive, sure, suspicious, vain, void, weary, worthy, etc.— all the adjectives take *'of* preposition* after them.

F.   Certain **Adjectives or Participles** which are followed by Preposition **'from' & 'for'**

114)   Man is entirely different ***from*** other animals in the utter hopelessness of his babyhood.

115)   Every mother is ***anxious for*** her child. He is ***celebrated for*** his last song.

116)   It is ***designed for*** gentlemen. I am not ***eager for*** it or any like that.

117)   He was ***destined for*** death for his continuous criminal acts.

118)   We were not ***eligible for*** the recruitment, they made it clear upon our face.

119)   Mumbai ***is famous for*** its textiles. Do you think you are ***fit for*** this thing?

120)   The Moors were ***famous for*** their learning and their skill in all kinds of industries.

121)   The gang was ***notorious for*** dacoity in that area since few decades.

122)   Coleridge's poetry is ***remarkable for*** the perfection of its execution.

❑   And thus, conspicuous, customary, eminent, good, grateful, penitent, prepared, proper, qualified, ready, sorry, sufficient, useful, jealous, etc. — all the above adjectives take **'for'** preposition after them.

Conjugation of Preposition with Verbs:

A. The Certain **Verbs** which are in most cases followed by Preposition **'to'**

123)   The boarders are ***accustomed to*** rise early.

124)   Camels are peculiarly ***adapted to*** life in the desert.

125)   Ivory readily ***adapts itself to*** the carver's art.

126)   The ancient Greeks, though born in warm climate, seem to have been much ***addicted to*** the bottle.

127)   Ambition does not always **_conduce to_** ultimate happiness.
128)   The African elephant is now **_confined to_** Central Asia.
129)   I am **_indebted to_** you **_for_** your help.
130)   A residence of eight years in Sri Lanka had **_inured_** his system **_to_** the tropical climate.

❑   And thus, accede, adhere, allot, allude, apologize, appoint, ascribe, aspire, assent, attain, attend, attribute, belong, conform, consent, contribute, lead, listen, object, occur, prefer, pretend, refer, revert, stoop, succumb, surrender, testify, yield, etc.— all the verbs take
'to' preposition after them.

B.   The Certain **_Verbs_** which are in most cases followed by Preposition **_'from'_**

131)   **_Abstain from_** drink & smoking. They are injurious to health.
132)   Suddenly it **_emerged from_** the cave & howled to startle all of us.
133)   He **_escaped from_** jail, but within hours he was sent back.
134)   It is **_excluded from_** the list. **_Preserve_** it **_from_** rotting.
135)   The income **_derived from_** the ownership of land is commonly called rent.
136)   The noise from downstairs **_prevented_** me **_from_** sleeping.
137)   Please **_protect_** us **_from_** their attack.
138)   She **_recoiled_** herself **_from_** their touch and ran very fast leaving them behind far.
139)   He has been **_recovering from_** fever after five days.
140)   Learn to **_refrain_** yourself from the bad company.

❑   And thus, accede, adhere, allot, allude, apologize, appoint, ascribe, aspire, assent, attain, attend, attribute, belong, conform, consent, contribute, lead, listen, object, occur, prefer, pretend, refer, revert, stoop, succumb, surrender, testify, yield, etc. — all the verbs take
'from' preposition after them.

C.   The Certain **_Verbs_** which are in most cases followed by Preposition **_'with'_**

141)   I am already **_acquainted with_** the latest developments of the situation.
142)   John was an **_associate_** professor **_with_** the Harvard University.
143)   I always **_associate_** the smell of baking **_with_** my childhood.

144)   He is closely **_associated_** in the public mind **_with_** his horror movies.
145)   I **_associate_** myself **_with_** his remarks. (Agree with)
146)   The holy tree is **_associated with_** scenes of goodwill & rejoicing.
147)   Her later work does not bear **_comparison with_** her earlier novels.
148)   The supporters of two leading political parties **_clashed with_** each other.
149)   The leaders **_clashed with_** the party members on the issue.
150)   The strike was **_coincided with_** the party conference.
151)   Her story **_coincided_** exactly **_with_** her brother's.
152)   They refused to **_comply with_** the new resolution.
153)   He was **_endowed with_** gifts fitted to win eminence in any field of human activity. She **_persevered with_** her violin lesson.
   ❑   And thus, condole, cope, correspond, credit, deluge, disagree, dispense, expostulate, fill, grapple, intrigue, meddle, part, quarrel, remonstrate, side, sympathize, trifle, vie, etc.— all the above verbs take **_'with'_** preposition after them.

D.   The Certain **_Verbs_** which are in most cases followed by Preposition **_'of'_**

154)   The convict is finally **_acquitted of_** all charges against him.
155)   **_Beware of_** coming danger and take steps accordingly.
156)   She **_boasts of_** her beauty and she doesn't know it never live long.
157)   You are **_complaining of_** what doesn't exist at all!
158)   A man who always **_connives at_** the faults **_of_** his children is their worst enemy.
159)   He **_died of_** a superman. The officer **_disapproved of_** all.
160)   The writer is evidently **_enamored of_** the subject.
161)   He **_healed of_** injury and enlisted his name for participant.
162)   Everyone must **_repent of_** his or her ill doings one day.
   ❑   And thus, despair, dispose, divest, dream, judge, taste, etc.— all the above verbs take **_'of'_** _preposition_ after them.

E.   The Certain **_Verbs_** which are in most cases followed by Preposition **_'for'_**

163)   Should you not **_atone for_** your crime?
164)   He spent the whole months **_canvassing for_** votes.
165)   People began to **_clamor for_** his resignation.

166)   He ***hopes for*** none to come forward to her help in her distress.

167)   The lady ***mourned for*** her husband's death and while alive she only quarreled.

168)   She ***pined for*** months after he'd gone. I feel ***sorry for*** him.

169)   We ***started for*** Kolkata and reached after ten hours only.

170)   We ***stipulated*** everything for the execution before long.

171)   Ravi ***sued*** Rakesh ***for*** the breach of contract made between them.

172)   It is natural in every man to ***wish for*** distinction.

173)   He ***yearns for*** nothing.

174)   The President ***called for*** an immediate ***cessation of*** hostilities among the communities in West India.

    F.   The following **verbs** take the preposition ***'in'***, after them:

175)   Isabella ***excelled in*** her unique performance on the stage.

176)   She has never been one to ***indulge in*** gossip.

177)   She was free to ***indulge in*** a little romantic day dreaming.

178)   She was ***involved in*** the publication of the book.

179)   How many vehicles were ***involved in*** the crash?

180)   You have ***involved*** me ***in*** a great deal of extra work.

181)   The cat appears to have ***originated in*** Egypt, or in the East.

182)   She ***persisted in*** her search for the truth.

183)   Why do you ***persist in*** blaming yourself for what happened?

184)   He ***persisted with*** his questioning.

185)   His name was ***enlisted in*** the panel for recruitment.

186)   In the classical age the ideal life of Hindu was ***divided into*** four stages of ashrams.

    G.   The following **verbs** take the preposition ***'on'***, ***'into'*** ***'from'*** or ***'by'*** after them:

187)   Don't ***comment on*** others, look to yourself.

188)   Who ***depends on*** you at home?

189)   So, you made a mistake, but there is no need to ***dwell on*** it.

190)   She didn't want to ***impose*** her values ***on*** her family.

191)   A new tax was ***imposed on*** fuel.

192)   He ***insisted on*** his innocence. (He insisted that he was innocent)

193)   We had ***resolved on*** making an early start.

194)   The government is ***trampling on*** the views of ordinary people.

195)   Don't ***trample on*** the flowers.

196)   She wouldn't let him ***trample over*** her any longer.
197)   The goat ***subsists on*** the coarsest of food.
198)   Old people often ***subsist on*** very small income.
199)   The sound of his telephone **intruded into** his dream.
200)   Alexander ***profited by*** the dissensions of the Punjab Rajas.
201)   ***Jugged by*** its results the policy of Hastings was eminently successful.

Exercise-3: **Pick out Prepositions & also their objects**:

a) A black cat sat in the corner of a room.
b) Mrs. Persome asked Mary about the silver candlesticks.
c) There's no going home till morning if this weather lasts.
d) Humpty Dumpty sat on a wall.
e) The boy runs across the road.
f) The traveler slept in the woods beneath a large tree.
g) The dog overturned the burning candle onto the table.
h) You must discuss with me regarding this matter.
i) Owing to acute hunger the man began to eat the leaves of the trees.
j) On went her old brown jacket; on went her brown locks of hair.
k) They rise with the morning lark, and labor till dark.
l) My grandmother sat by the window, looked out & told us ghost tales.

Answers to Exercise-3: **Pick out Prepositions & also their objects**

a) A black cat sat **in** *the corner* of a room.
b) Mrs. Persome asked Mary **about** *the silver candlesticks*.
c) There's no going home **till** *morning* if this weather lasts.
d) Humpty Dumpty sat **on** *a wall*.
e) The boy runs **across** *the road*.
f) The traveler slept in the woods **beneath** *a large tree*.
g) The dog overturned the burning candle **onto** *the table*.
h) You must discuss with me **regarding** *this matter*.
i) Owing to acute hunger the man began to eat the leaves **of** *the trees*.
j) On went her old brown jacket; on went her brown locks **of** *hair*.
k) They rise with the morning lark, and labor **till** *dark*.
l) My grandmother sat **by** *the window*, looked out & told us ghost tales.

(The bold lettered words are the prepositions, when the underlined are their objects, objects to the prepositions)

Exercise-4: **<u>Fill in the blanks with appropriate Prepositions</u>**:
a) He was born _____ a small town _____the district of Dakshin Dinajpur.
b) We started ________ 5 o'clock _____ the morning.
c) Distribute this _________ Om & Nicky.
d) He refused to take less _______fifteen rupees for the soap.
e) Here is the book that you asked _________.
f) Who is the person you are speaking _______?
g) Distribute the mangoes ________the boys.
h) She wants to start _____seven o'clock in the morning.
i) She has been there ________ three o'clock _____ the afternoon.
j) It has been raining _______ two days.
k) The girl has been suffering _______ 12th instant.
l) She began to write poems _______his boyhood.
m) He will be in the office _________tomorrow.
n) I didn't see Mr. Lahiri ________________three days.
o) Here is a chair to sit _______________.
p) The man has a reputation _________honesty. He has the reputation ________being a good policeman.
q) She fell victim _________ cholera. The victims ______cholera were immediately sent to a hospital.
r) He supplied cloths _______the poor. The poor were supplied ________the cloths
s) We talk ______literature. They talk ________something else. I shall talk ______my daughter ______her attendance in college.
t) The boy is negligent ______whatever he does. He is also negligent _______his duties.

Answer to Exercise-4: **<u>Fill in the blanks with appropriate Prepositions</u>**:
a) He was born _____ a small town _____the district of Dakshin Dinajpur. (at, in)
b) We started ________ 5 o'clock _____ the morning. (at, in)
c) Distribute this _________ Om & Nicky. (between)
d) He refused to take less _______fifteen rupees for the soap. (than)
e) Here is the book that you asked _________. (for)
f) Who is the person you are speaking _______? (to)
g) Distribute the mangoes ________the boys. (among)
h) She wants to start _____seven o'clock in the morning. (at)

i)   She has been there _________ three o'clock ______ the afternoon. (by, in)
j)   It has been raining _______ two days. (for)
k)   The girl has been suffering _______ 12th instant. (from)
l)   She began to write poems _______his boyhood. (in)
m) He will be in the office _________tomorrow. (by)
n) I didn't see Mr. Lahiri _________________three days. (for)
o) Here is a chair to sit _______________. (on)
p) The man has a reputation _________honesty. He has the reputation ________being a good policeman. (For, of)
q) She fell victim _________ cholera. The victims _______cholera were immediately sent to a hospital. (of, to)
r) He supplied cloths _______the poor. The poor were supplied _________the cloths (to, with)
s) We talk ______literature. They talk ________something else. I shall talk ______my daughter ______her attendance in college. (about, of, to, about)
t) The boy is negligent ______whatever he does. He is also negligent _______his duties. (of, in)

Exercise-5: **Distinguish the prepositions from adverbs in the following sentences**:

1) Come down. (as adverb)

2) We sailed down the river. (as preposition)

3) The man walked round the house. (as preposition)

4) He sat on a stool. (as preposition)

5) The carriage moved on. (as adverb)

6) The soldiers passed by. (as adverb)

7) The man turned round. (as adverb)

8) We all went in. (as adverb)

9) He is in the room. (as preposition)

10) He hid behind the door. (as preposition)

11) I left him behind. (as adverb)

12) She sat by the cottage door. (as preposition)

13) The path leads through the woods. (as preposition)

14) I have read the book through. (as adverb)

15) The storm is raging without. (as adverb)

16) We cannot live without water. (as preposition)

3. Conjunctions, Classification & Functions

The Chapter includes two main ways of Classification of Conjunctions which are based on **Forms** and **Functions** of the conjunctions; and then their sub-divisions. Firstly, Conjunctions may be divided in this following two ways; as into:

    A. Simple, Correlative & Compound (based on forms or construction of the conjunctions); and as,

    B. Coordinating & Subordinating Conjunctions (based on their functions).

Again, the second group of classification includes further sub-division of conjunctions, based on **meanings**; as, the Coordinate Conjunctions are further sub-divided into:

    a) Cumulative,
    b) Alternative,
    c) Adversative &
    d) Illative

And the Subordinate Conjunctions which generally join subordinate clauses, do the following functions, and their sub-divisions based upon. They may join a clause that—

a) **Forms a subject or object, as a noun does**, to the main verb,

b) **Qualifies a noun or a pronoun preceding**, popularly known as antecedent,

c) **Modify or add meaning to verb, adjective or to another adverb**. Doing so, sub-ordinate conjunctions may refer again- time, purpose, cause, condition, result, comparison, and contrast (to form sub-ordinate adverbial clauses in the sentence.)

Now, read them in details.

Definition: The word or the part of speech that join two words, or phrases or clauses of equal or unequal rank, is called a conjunction. Read below the first group of Classification of Conjunctions.

Simple, Correlative & Compound Conjunctions

Based on formation or structure, the Conjunctions may be of the following kinds:

Study of Adverbs, Prepositions, Conjunctions & Interjections

> A) Simple Conjunctions,
> B) Correlative Conjunctions, &
> C) Compound or Phrase Conjunctions.

A. **Simple Conjunctions:** The simple conjunctions are single word conjunctions; as, *and, but, or, therefore, still, yet, only,* etc.

The following sentences include the examples of Simple Conjunctions (conjunctions of single word) used in them:

- We carved not a line, **and** we raised not a stone.
- Is that story true **or** false?
- The man is poor, **but** honest.
- I was annoyed, **still** I kept quiet.
- Something certainly fell in; **for** I heard a splash.
- We arrived **after** you had gone.
- I would die **before** I lied.
- She must weep, **lest** she die.
- **As** he was not there, I spoke to his brother.
- You will be late **unless** you hurry.
- He is slow **but,** he is sure.
- He is richer **than** I am.
- He was sorry **after** he had done it.

B. **Correlative Conjunctions:** Some conjunctions are used in pair or double in the sentence with the both parts or clauses of the sentence; as,

> 1. both—and,
> 2. not only—but also,
> 3. whether—or,
> 4. either—or,
> 5. neither—nor,
> 6. though—yet, etc.

The use of Correlative Conjunctions:

- We do **both** love **and** honor him.
- **Not only** is he foolish, **but also** obstinate.
- **Either** take it **or** leave the place.
- It is **neither** useful **nor** pleasing.
- **Whether** he'll go **or** I have to.
- I do not care **whether** you go **or** stay.
- **Though** he is suffering much pain, **yet** he does not complain.
- **Though** he worked hard, **yet** he failed in the test.

C. **Compound or Phrase Conjunctions:** The conjunctions which consist of two or more words, when a phrase is used as a conjunction in the sentence, is known as the **Compound or Phrase Conjunctions**; as, *as well as, inasmuch as, as soon as, in order that, even if, as if,* etc. (They are used with a single part or clause in the sentence. Study the examples.)

The following sentences consist the examples of Compound Conjunctions, used in them:

- o   The notice was published *in order that* all might know the facts.
- o   I will forgive you *on condition that* you do not repeat the offence.
- o   Such an act would not be kind *even if* it were just.
- o   He saved some bread *so that* he should not go hungry on the morrow.
- o   You can borrow the book *provided that* you return it soon.
- o   He walks *as though* he is slightly lame.
- o   I must refuse your request, *inasmuch as* I believe it unreasonable.
- o   He took off his coat *as soon as* he entered the house.
- o   He looks *as if* he were weary.

* All the above are examples of **compound conjunctions (written in bold). And at the same time, they are** the **sub-ordinate conjunctions**, if we consider the second group of classification, as they join dependent clause with the main.

* There are many *compound conjunctions* which are also the *coordinating conjunctions* in function or use.

* So, a conjunction (**Simple, Correlative** or **Compound**) in form or structure of one group may be either of the **Co-ordinate** or **Sub-ordinate** too. Regarding this, there is not any contradiction to use. [Like, a man may be a doctor, a father and a husband.]

o The following Correlative & Compound Conjunctions are the **Co-ordinating Conjunctions** too. And thus, you may also find out the rest.

- o   *Both* Prakash *and* Pravat were absent from the school.
- o   Prakash *as well as* Pravat were absent from school.

Coordinating & Subordinating Conjunctions

Classification of Conjunctions, based on Functions

That joins together words, phrases or clauses **of equal rank or importance**.	i.e. **and, or, then, but, else, however, therefore, still, yet, for, only, either...or, neither...nor, as well as** etc.

That joins a clause to another clause where **one clause is dependent** on main clause.	**Before, after, because, that,** than, if, **whether,** though, although, till, unless, as, when, where, while **&** other **wh. words** etc.

According to function or use, the conjunctions are again of mainly two kinds:

       A. Coordinating Conjunctions, &
       B. Subordinating Conjunctions.

The following are the main four Functions or divisions of Coordinating conjuncts, according to their meanings. These are as,

A. **Cumulative or Copulative**

- That simply joins two words, phrases, clauses of equal rank of action or names.
- And, also, too, as well as, both—and, not only—but also, etc.

Of the above, some of Cumulative are also the **Simple Conjunctions** regarding their form out of single word; as, **'and', 'also', 'too'**, etc.

While, **'both—and, not only—but also**—are the examples of **Corelative Conjunctions** (regarding form), and

'as well as'—an example of **Phrase Conjunction**.

Examples of Cumulative conjunctions in the sentences:
o   We carved not a line, *and* we raised not a stone.
o   God made the country *and* man, made town.
o   Two *and* two make four. Four *and* four make eight.
o   Bread *and* milk is a wholesome food.
o   Bed *and* bedsheet I bought.
o   Vishal *and* Virat are good bowlers. (Vishal is a good bowler and Virat is a good bowler.)
o   I like tea, *also* I like coffee. I like *both* tea *and* coffee.
o   You like her, I *too*.
o   He is a teacher *as well as* a writer.
o   Sam is *not only* a good player *but also* an excellent singer.

B. **Alternative or Disjunctive**
▪   That joins two parts or clauses referring a selection or a choice between two alternatives or two different things.
➢   Either...or, neither...nor, whether—or, or, neither, else, etc.

Like the above, here too, some of Alternative Conjunctions are also the **Simple Conjunctions** regarding their form out of single word; as, '**whether**', '**or**', **neither**, '**else**', etc.
While, 'either—or, neither—nor, whether—or — are the examples of **Corelative Conjunctions**.

Examples of Alternative conjunctions in the Sentences:
o   She must weep, *or* she will die.
o   *Either* he is mad *or* he feigns madness.
o   Is that story true *or* false?
o   *Neither* a borrower *nor* a lender be.
o   We can travel by land *or* water.
o   They toil not, *neither* do they spin.
o   *Either* you are mistaken *or* I am.
o   Walk quickly, *else* you will not overtake him.
o   I must go *whether* he go *or* not go.

C. **Adversative or Contrast**
▪   The conjunctions that join sentences or clauses that is opposed to or the opposite of what has been said.
➢   Still, yet, only, but, however, nevertheless, though—yet, etc.

Of the above, some of Adversative are also the **Simple Conjunctions** regarding their form out of single word; as, '**still**', '**yet**', '**only**', '**but**', '**however**', '**nevertheless**', etc.

While, '**though—yet** —is an example of **Corelative Conjunction.**

Examples of Adversative Conjunctions in the sentences:
- Our hoard is little, **but** our hearts are great.
- The man is poor, **but** honest. (The man is poor, but he is honest.)
- He is slow **but,** he is sure.
- I was annoyed, **still** I kept quiet.
- I would come; **only** that I am engaged.
- He was all right; **only** he was fatigued.
- He is a rogue, **yet** he is my brother.
- He is a poor; **however**, he manages his family well.
- **Nevertheless**, the boy was poor; the strength of his mind was amendable.
- **Though** she suffered a lot, **yet** she uttered no words.

D. Illative (the conjunctions of inference)
- That denotes or express an inference (the conjunction that joins a clause or sentence that forms an opinion, based on what you already know.)
  - Therefore, for, so, then, so then etc.

Of the above, some of Illative are also the **Simple Conjunctions** regarding their form out of single word; as, '**therefore**', '**for**', '**so**', '**then**', etc., and '**so then**'—is an example of **Compound Conjunction**.

The use of Illative conjunctions in the sentences:
- He had been suffering from fever; **therefore**, he was absent in the meeting.
- Something certainly fell in; **for** I heard a splash.
- All precautions must have been neglected; **for** the plague spread rapidly.
- He worked very hard; **so**, he gained his reward.
- He finished his task; **then** he returned home.
- All performed their roles; **so, then** it was her turn to act in accordance.

Functions of Subordinating Conjunctions

Sub-ordinate conjunctions **join the sub-ordinate clauses**, which may be **Noun Clause**, **Relative** or **Adjective Clause**, or **Adverbial Clause.** Read the following sentences.

1) *When he will come* is uncertain.
2) *Why my friend failed* is known to all.
3) I know *where he lives*.
4) I know *that he is ill*.
5) I know the **boy** who did it.
6) He was a brilliant **player** who did a hat trick taking wickets in the last series.
7) This is the **place** where I was born.
8) Do you know the **reason** why he failed in the Exam?

To be noted: In the above, with the first four sentences (from 1 to 4), certain clauses are joined by some certain pronouns or linkers, certain 'wh-'words or by 'that', and we have Sub-ordinate Noun clauses.

In the next four sentences (5 to 8), the clauses are again joined by some relative pronouns or adverbs, so called 'wh adjunctive pronouns or adverbs', and we have Sub-ordinate Relative or Adjective clauses.

Like the above, there are certain conjunctions, do almost the same functions, do join clauses; especially, sub-ordinate adverbial clauses in the sentence.

Relating adverbial clause, a sub-ordinate conjunction does the following functions, besides join the clauses: Read the chart.

Adverbial Functions of Sub-ordinate Conjunctions

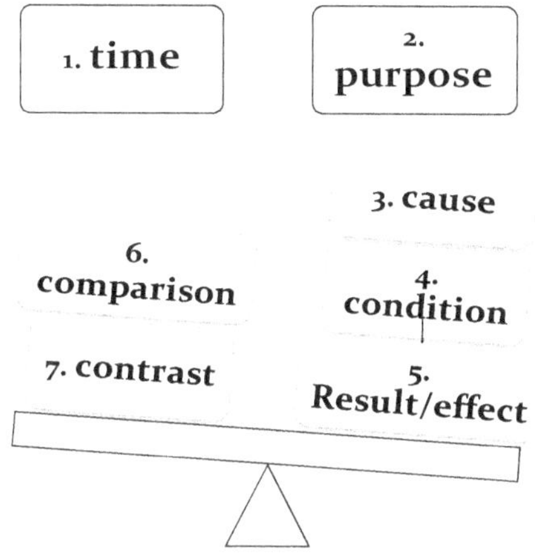

Conjunctions which do the adverbial functions

Time	**after,** before, **since,** as soon as, **while,** until, **as,** so long as, till..
Purpose	**in order** that, **lest, so that,** that..
Cause	**because,** since, **as..**
Condition	**provided,** supposing, **unless, as, if,** whether..
Result/Effect	**so...that**
Comparison	**Than, that,** as...as
Contrast	**though,** although, **however,** even if.

Let's study them now application in the sentences; <u>**how do they do their functions in the sentences:**</u>

❏ <u>Sub-ordinate Conjunctions, denoting-</u>

1) Time:
o   We arrived ***after*** you had gone.

- I waited *till* the train arrived.
- *When* you are called, you must come in at once.
- Do not go *before* I come.
- We got into the port *before* the storm came on.
- My grandfather died *before* I was born.
- I will stay *until* you return.
- I would die *before* I lied.
- Many things have happened *since* I saw you.
- He returned home *after* he had gone.
- She returned *as soon as* her husband reached there.
- *While* I was reading a book, she was cooking for us all.
- *As* (when) you called, I came to you every time.
- She continued her act with the villain *as long as* she could and the police reached in time.

2) Purpose:
- She must weep, *lest* she die. Let her sorrow flow, thereby.
- We tried hard *in order that* it spin.
- He is intelligent, *so* he feigned madness.
- She feigned madness, *so that* she saved herself from that danger.
- We travel by land or water *so that* we can reach another place.
- We eat *so that* we may live. We eat *that* we can live.
- He held my hand *lest* I should fall.

3) Cause or Reason:
- I cannot give you any money, *because* I have none.
- *Since* you wish it, it shall be done.
- I shall be vexed *if* you do that. He may enter *as* he is a friend.
- *As* he was not there, I spoke to his brother.
- I did not come *because* you did not call me.
- He deserved to succeed, *as* he had worked very hard.

4) Condition:
- You will not succeed *unless* you work harder.
- You will get the prize *if* you deserve it.
- He fled *lest* he should be killed.
- Grievance cannot be redressed *unless* they are known.
- You will be late *unless* you hurry.
- He asked *whether* he might have a holiday.
- Give me to drink; *else* I shall die of thirst.
- *If* I feel any doubt, I ask.
- I shall go, *whether* you come or not.
- *Unless* you tell me the truth, I shall punish you.
- He will sure to come *if* you invite him.

5) Result/effect/Consequence:
- He was sorry *after* he had done it.
- He was so tired *that* he could scarcely stand.

6) Comparison:
- He is richer *than* I am.
- Tom runs faster *than* Harry.
- The earth is larger *than* the moon.

7) Contrast / Concession:
- Our hoard is little, *but* our hearts are great.
- The man is poor, *but* honest. (The man is poor, but he is honest.)
- He is slow, *but* he is sure. I was annoyed, still I kept quiet.
- I would come; *only* that I am engaged.
- He was all right; *only* he was fatigued.
- I hear *that* your brother is in London.

Conjunctions, how distinguished from Relative Pronouns, Relative Adverbs, & Prepositions:

- *Study them carefully:*

1. This is the house *that* Jack built. (*Relative Pronoun*)
2. This is the place *where* he was murdered. (*Relative Adverb*)
3. Take this *and* give that. (*Conjunction*)
4. He may enter *as* he is a friend. (*Conjunction*)

- **In sentence 1, *'that'*** is a relative pronoun, as it is used in place of noun **'house'** and it is relative, as it <u>introduces a relative or adjective clause</u> 'that jack built'. Besides, it joins the two clauses.

- **In sentence 2, *'where'*** is an adverb, denoting 'a place' and it is relative adverb, as it has <u>introduced a relative or adjective clause</u> 'where he was murdered. Besides, it joins the two clauses.

- **In sentence 3, *'and'*** is a coordinate cumulative conjunction, that joins two independent parts of a sentence. It is a Co-ordinate conjunction as it joins two clauses of equal rank or independent.

- **In sentence 4, *'as'*** is a sub-ordinate conjunction, being closely attached to a sub-ordinate or dependent clause, joins two clauses of a sentence.

- **Certain Words, used both as Prepositions & Conjunctions**

Preposition	Conjunction
1. Stay *till* Monday.	1. We shall stay here *till* you return.
2. I have not met him *since* Monday.	2. We shall go *since* you desire it.
3. He died *for* his country.	3. I must stay here, *for* such is my duty.
4. The dog ran *after* the cat.	4. We came *after* they had left.
5. Everybody *but* Govind was present.	5. He tried, *but* did not succeed.
6. He stood *before* the painting.	6. Look *before* you leap.

o **Exercise-1: Distinguish** *as <u>Adverb</u>, <u>Preposition</u>, or <u>Conjunction</u>, out of the italicized words in the following sentences*:

→ He came *before* me.
→ He came two hours *before*.
→ He came *before* I left.
→ Have you ever seen him *since* Monday?
→ I have not seen him *since* he was a child.
→ Man wants *but* little here below.
→ He yearns for nothing *but* money.
→ We shall go, *but* you will remain.
→ He arrived *after* the meeting was adjourned.
→ He arrived soon *after*.

Special attention to the use of Some Conjunctions

o Actually, every word and every part of speech has special uses which are unique and different from others. However, we use the term '*special attention*' for some. It is due to, to draw our extra attention to them. You will read some words which may seem to be a pronoun, preposition, or an adverb, when actually they are doing the work of a conjunction in the sentences. Here, out of conjunctions, they are:

(1) **Since:** *it means 'since and after the time'; it also means 'as, for' referring reason or cause; as,*

- Many things have happened **since** I left school.
- I have not seen him **since** that unfortunate event happened.
- **Since** you wish it, it shall be done.
- **Since** you will not work, you shall not eat.

(2) **Or:** *is used to mean 'alternate between two', 'otherwise', 'nearly equivalent to'; as,*
- You must work **or** starve.
- Your purse **or** your life.
- You may take this book **or** that one.
- The violin or fiddle has become the leading instrument of the modern **or**chestra.
- You must hasten **or** night will overtake us.
- The troops were not wanting in strength **or** courage, but they were badly fed.

(3) **If:** *is used to mean 'on the condition or supposition that', 'admitting that', 'whether', 'whenever' & also to express 'wish or surprise'; as,*
- *If* he is there, I'll meet him.
- *If* that is so, I am content.
- *If* I am blunt, I am at least honest.
- *Though* I am poor, *yet* I am honest.
- I asked him *if* he would help me.
- I wonder *if* he will come.
- *If* I feel any doubt I inquire.
- *If* I only knew!

(4) **Than:** *as a conjunction follows adjectives & adverbs in the comparative degree; as,*
- Wisdom is better *than* rubies.
- I am better acquainted with the country *than* you are.
- I would rather suffer *than* that you should want.

(5) **That:** *is used to express 'a reason or cause', 'purpose or in order that', 'consequence, result or effect'; as,*
- Not *that* I loved Caesar less, but *that* I loved Rome more.
- He was annoyed *that* he was contradicted.
- We sow, *that* we may reap.
- He kept quiet *that* the dispute might cease.
- I am so tired *that* I cannot go.
- He bled so profusely *that* he died.
- He was so tired *that* he could scarcely stand.

(6) **Lest:** *as sub-ordinate conjunction it expresses negative purpose and means 'in order that...not', 'for fear that', as,*
- Love not sleep, *lest* thou come to poverty.
- Do not be idle, *lest* you come to want.
- He fled *lest* he should be killed.
- I was alarmed *lest* we should be wrecked.

(7) **While:** *to mean 'during the time that' 'as long as', 'at the same time that', 'whereas'; as,*
- *While* he was sleeping, a thief entered his house.
- *While* there is life, there is hope.
- The girls sang *while* the boys played football.
- *While* he found fault, he also praised.
- *While* I have no money to spend, you have nothing to spend on.
- *While* this is true of some, it is not true of all.

(8) **Only:** *as a conjunction, means 'except that'; as,*
- A very pretty woman, *only* she squints a little.
- The day is pleasant, *only* rather cold.
- He does well, *only* that he is nervous at the start.
- I would go with you, *only* I have no money.

(9) **Except / without:** *means 'unless',*
- *Except* you repent (unless), you'll not feel peace at mind.
- *Except* a man is reasonable, he is not a man of modern world.
- I shall not go *without* you do.

(10) **Because, for, since:** *of these three conjunctions, 'because' denotes 'the closest cause' 'for' denotes 'weakest reason', while 'since' denotes the cause between because & for; as,*
- He couldn't attend the meeting, *because* he was ill. (Strong reason)
- *Since* you say so, I must believe it. (Reason is enough but not strong as denotes by 'because')
- He gives lecture, *for* he is a teacher. (Weakest reason; anyone can give lecture)

Exercise-2: Join each pair of sentences with a suitable conjunction:
- My brother is well. My sister is ill.
- He sells mangoes. He sells oranges.
- He did not succeed. He worked hard.

- Ruma reads for pleasures. Ritwika reads for profit.
- He is poor. He is contented.
- The sheep are grazing. The oxen are grazing.
- I lost the prize. I tried my best.
- I like him. He is dangerous.
- I ran fast. I missed the train.
- He remained cheerful. He has been wounded.
- I have a cricket bat. I have a set of stumps.

4. Interjections & Examples

INTERJECTION

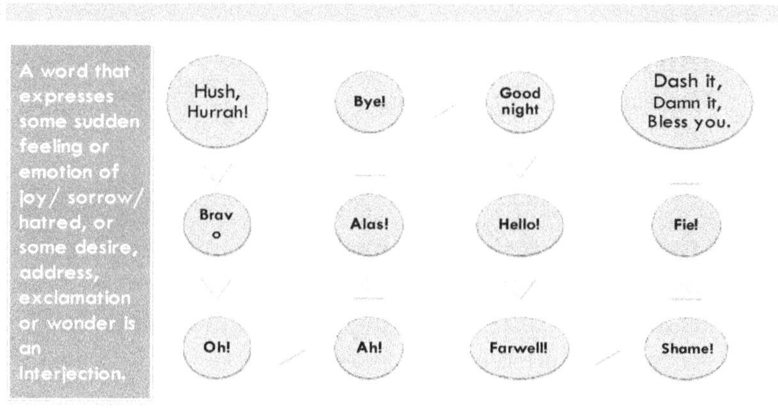

☐ A word that expresses some sudden feeling or emotion of joy/ sorrow/ hatred, or some desire, address, exclamation or wonder is an Interjection.

           o   The Uses of Interjections:

- **Alas!** He has lost his watch.
- **Hurrah!** We have won the trophy.
- **Hallow!** How are you?
- **Hush!** (silence/be quiet/shut up) there is someone.
- **Bravo!** You have done it.
- **Oh!** I forget it.
- **Ah!** It's very tasty.
- **Bye!** Bye, O great soul, forever.

- **<u>Good night</u>**, see you tomorrow morning.
- **<u>Farwell!</u>** My pleasure with thy departure.
- **<u>Shame!</u>** You have done so mean.
- **<u>Fie!</u>** You have done this.
- **<u>Dash it</u>**! Who has done these! (To show that you are annoyed about something)
- **<u>Damn</u>**! If I'll apologize. / **<u>Damn</u>**! Who the rascal is? (To refuse to do something; to show you are surprised)
- **<u>Bless you</u>**, you would be a great man.

Note: An interjection that expresses wish, desire, calling or address, may also be used with full stop (.) in the sentence. The use of exclamation (!) is not bound to be used always with the interjection, though generally that may be used.

○ **An Interjection may express—**

(1) **Joy & amusement; as,**
- **Hurrah!** We all have passed.
- **Huzzah!** Finally, it is done.
- **Ha!** Today is a great day.

(2) **Grief or sorrow; as,**
- **Oh!** What a great loss that would be.
- **Ah!** She has departed without meeting me.
- **Alas!** My maternal uncle is dead. Alas! I am undone.
- **Alas & alack!** We had missed our bus.

(3) **Surprise or wonder; as,**
- **Ha!** (Also: **hah**) It serves you right! / **Ha!** I knew he was hiding something. So, he is the Peter! (Used to express when one is surprised or pleased)
- **What!** He is Peter! The writer of the book.
- **Ah,** there you are! **Ah,** this coffee is good. **Ah well,** better luck next time. **Ah,** but that may not be true. (Used to express surprise, pleasure, admiration, sympathy)

(4) **Applaud or Approval; as,**
- **Bravo!** You have scored the winning goal.
- **Well done,** John. Here's a biscuit for you.
- **Good Gracious**: I hope you didn't mind my phoning you. Good gracious, no, of course not! (used as to say something by name of God)

(5) Hatred or abhorrence; Disgust or Ridicule; as,

- **Fie** upon you, you devilish fool! (to express distaste, disgust, outrage)
- **Shame!** She is so cute & wounded! (to express sympathy, but also 'disgust); **For shame!** Stop please.
- **Stuff!** Do not do that. (Disapproving); Stuff! Sure, I do not agree with you.
- **Pooh!** = It stinks! Pooh! (express disgust to a bad smell)
- **Tush!** It is suitable for you. The slap of God! (contempt or rebuke)
- **Tut-tut,** I expected better of you! (to express disapproval off something)

(6) Wish, desire or address (call someone); as,

- **Welcome home!** Welcome to Oxford! Welcome to central jail! (As a greeting to tell, you are happy or pleased of)
- **Ho!** Who is there? (For calling, but also express disgust); **Ho,** it is suitable for him!
- **Hello!** Who are you ask me that?
- **Hi**= hello: Hi guys! Hi there! How're you doing?

(7) Attention; as,

- **Hark!** I hear a step on the stairs! (Used to tell somebody to listen)
- **Hush!** The teacher is coming.
- **Lo!** Something wrong is going on there. (Drawing attention to a surprised thing)
- **Hist!** Someone is talking to the woman. (To draw attention to something)

(8) Expressing doubt; as,

- **Hum! / Hmm! / Humph! Hem!** = **Humph**, is that true? (Express doubt or disapproval)
- **Bosh,** is it be!

Interjections are used to express some sudden feeling or emotion. It will be noticed that that they are not grammatically related to other words in a sentence.

(9) As idiom 'lo and behold':

- **A**s soon as we out, _lo and behold_, it began to rain.

o **Certain Phrases are used as Interjections:**
   There are certain phrases which are used as the interjections in the sentences. Carefully study the sentences:
   - **Ah me!** You hate your life long.
   - **Well done friend!** You have done excellent.
   - **Good bye!** We don't know will we meet again?
   - **O dear me!** What you have done.
   - **Bad luck to it!** He tried his best yet.
   - **Good gracious!** How one can do this alone.
   - **Good heavens!** Who can do it?
   - **Well, to be sure!** It is he has done this job.
   - **For shame!** Leave me alone.

o **Certain Verbs or other Parts of Speech, used as Interjections:**
   There are _certain moods of verbs_ or _parts of speech_ that are used as the interjections in the sentences:

a) **Imperative:**
   - **Hear!** What a song she sings.
   - **Hear! Hear!** What a sound it is. (_applause_)
   - **See!** What a beautiful sight, ripple of light in thee.

b) **Subjunctive:**
   - _Would that I had_ the wings of a dove!
   - _If I would have_ billions in my little purse!
   - _If she the young Kajol would be,_ my eternal love! Perhaps, perhaps then, I would be the happiest in the world.
   (Thus, a whole sentence may be used to express the wish of the speaker and is expressed by the subjunctive mood of the verb.)

c) **By infinitive:**
   - **To think** that I should have played the match!
   - **To say** that I fell in love, first or last, is the worth least words!

d) **Adjective:**
   - **Strange!** She went there.
   - **Shocking!** How she can say so.

e) **Adjective+ Noun:**

- **Dreadful sight!** I can't explain.
- **Foolish fellow!** Or how one can behave before sure death.
- **What a mess!** Who can say here live a ward?

f) **Adverb:**
- **How** vary kind of you! If you didn't do, I fell in indomitable trouble. **How** wonderful!
- **How** beautiful!
- **How** awful is her love for my purse!

g) A full sentence with a pronoun: What a sad thing **it** is!
h) A full sentence with a conjunction: **If** I could see her once more!

o **Certain 'Wh' word with the main verb, used as Interjections:**
Sometimes while expressing strong emotion in rush, Auxiliary verb with Subject is left out, and only main verb is used, and sometimes with a 'wh' word; as,
- **Reached!** When?
- **Murdered!** How?
- **Why cry!** And for the man who has already forgotten you?
- **Why wait and spoil life!** Waiting for nothing come readymade.
- **Why go there!** You didn't tell it before.
- **What said!** I can't remember like that anything.
- **How reached!** And alone!
- **Wow!** But where it happened. /**Where happened!**

Note: thus, we can express interjections in various ways than till mentioned, for interjections are not only words but it includes sounds various to count, i.e., unending.

Exercise: <u>Study the examples and note what they express: write so in brackets.</u>
a. *Alas* for the evil day!
b. *Shame* upon you!
c. *Oh!* What fine things these are.
d. *Oh!* I forgot.
e. *Oh,* that he were present!
f. *Nonsense!* Just get lost from here.
g. *Hush!* Someone is coming towards us.
h. *What noise* is this?

i. *Fie* upon the traitor!
j. *Foolish fellow*! How could they do that!

<u>Answers</u>

a. *Alas* for the evil day! (Sorrow or grief)
b. *Shame* upon you! (contempt)
c. *Oh!* What fine things these are. (praise)
d. *Oh!* I forgot. (Express sorry, feel sorry)
e. *Oh,* that he were present! (wonder)
f. *Nonsense!* Just get lost from here. (abhorrence)
g. *Hush!* Someone is coming towards us. (Drawing attention)
h. *What* noise is this? (Expressing surprise)
i. *Fie* upon the traitor! (contempt/hatred)
j. *Foolish fellow*! How could they do that! (contempt & wonder)

About Mr. Peter

Mr. Peter is a penname of the writer, an Indian and a teacher in West Bengal. Most of his academic works are the products of his professional career what he held over twenty years and continuing… Mr. Peter loves to publish his books in the self-publishing platforms, like Amazon (worldwide) and notionpress.com (India). For this, Peter heartily pays his gratitude to Amazon, notionpress.com and for marketing to Flipkart, Amazon & different social media. Presently, Mr. Peter's books are available in 3 formats—eBook, Paperback & Hardcover. Mr. Peter's books which are published at Notion Press Pvt. Ltd., Chennai, are available to buy on **notionpress.com, Flipkart**, **Amazon**.in

Discounts, promotions, etc. are available in all platforms. However, if one seeks special offers for marketing or wants to give bulk order, s/he may visit only to notionpress.com (type Mr. Peter in the search box, and use following **Coupon Codes:** (If not work, for the current status, one may contact by https://www.facebook.com/profile.php?id=100081822070172 or (5) Books Campaigns, Free Coupons, Learning English Grammar & Composition | Facebook

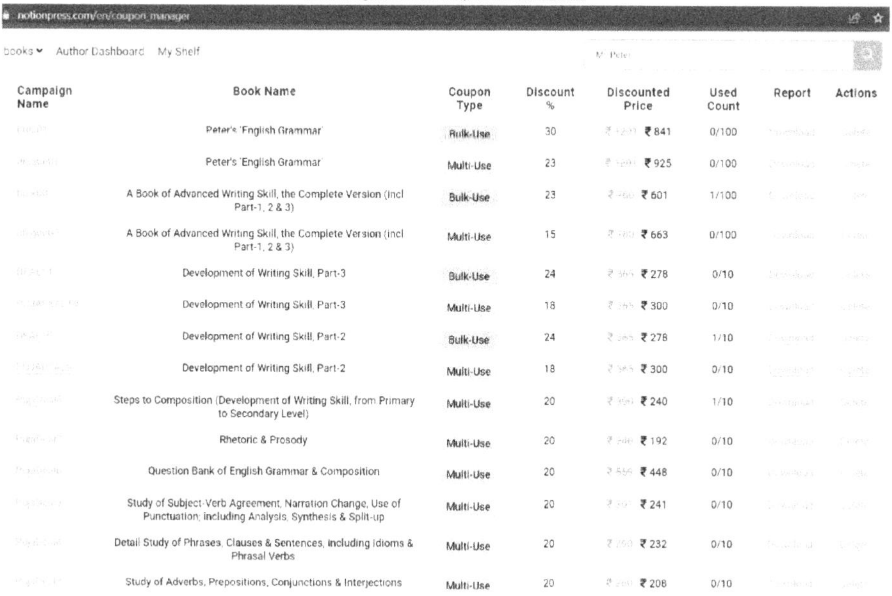

Campaign Name	Book Name	Coupon Type	Discount %	Discounted Price	Used Count	Report	Actions
	Peter's 'English Grammar'	Bulk-Use	30	₹ 841	0/100		
	Peter's 'English Grammar'	Multi-Use	23	₹ 925	0/100		
	A Book of Advanced Writing Skill, the Complete Version (incl Part-1, 2 & 3)	Bulk-Use	23	₹ 601	1/100		
	A Book of Advanced Writing Skill, the Complete Version (incl Part-1, 2 & 3)	Multi-Use	15	₹ 663	0/100		
	Development of Writing Skill, Part-3	Bulk-Use	24	₹ 278	0/10		
	Development of Writing Skill, Part-3	Multi-Use	18	₹ 300	0/10		
	Development of Writing Skill, Part-2	Bulk-Use	24	₹ 278	1/10		
	Development of Writing Skill, Part-2	Multi-Use	18	₹ 300	0/10		
	Steps to Composition (Development of Writing Skill, from Primary to Secondary Level)	Multi-Use	20	₹ 240	1/10		
	Rhetoric & Prosody	Multi-Use	20	₹ 192	0/10		
	Question Bank of English Grammar & Composition	Multi-Use	20	₹ 448	0/10		
	Study of Subject-Verb Agreement, Narration Change, Use of Punctuation; including Analysis, Synthesis & Split-up	Multi-Use	20	₹ 241	0/10		
	Detail Study of Phrases, Clauses & Sentences, including Idioms & Phrasal Verbs	Multi-Use	20	₹ 232	0/10		
	Study of Adverbs, Prepositions, Conjunctions & Interjections	Multi-Use	20	₹ 208	0/10		

* 9 7 9 8 8 8 7 0 4 5 3 2 0 *